MARYLAND AND VIRGINIA CONVICT RUNAWAYS, 1725 - 1800

A Survey of English Sources

Peter Wilson Coldham

Copyright © 2012
Peter Wilson Coldham
All rights reserved. No part of this publication may be
reproduced in any form or by any means, including
electronic reproduction or reproduction via the Internet,
except by permission of the publisher.

Published by Genealogical Publishing Company
3600 Clipper Mill Rd., Suite 260
Baltimore, Maryland 21211-1953

ISBN 978-0-8063-1891-2
Library of Congress Catalog Card Number: 2011939400

Made in the United States of America

INTRODUCTION

Since the first attempt in 1998 to provide a comprehensive account of the convicts who were condemned to serve a period of forced labour in the American colonies it has proved difficult to keep pace with the flood of companion volumes about the history and genealogy of those so condemned. The data now presented in this book aims to complete the final chapter of the story by setting out a guide to all the official and newspaper sources so far traced and made available online in English and transatlantic records listing all the felons known to have been shipped to Maryland and Virginia from 1614 onwards.

The following volumes/CDs which have been published under my name include all the so-called convict runaways so far identified:

The Complete Book of Emigrants in Bondage 1614-1775: Genealogical Publishing Co., Inc., 1992.

Supplement to The Complete Book of Emigrants in Bondage 1614-1775: Genealogical Publishing Co., Inc., 1992.

The King's Passengers to Maryland and Virginia: Family Line Publications, 1997.

More Emigrants in Bondage 1614-1775: Genealogical Publishing Co., Inc., 2002.

The CD entitled *British Emigrants in Bondage 1614-1788* includes all the above titles and is available from Genealogical Publishing Co., Inc.

In an introduction in 2003 to the subject of identifying Virginia runaways Kenneth Howell perspicaciously commented: "As the academic community becomes further inundated in the vast quagmire of the world-wide web, scholars are introduced to a barrage of websites that often promise more than they actually deliver.... [there is] a plethora of poorly researched and awkwardly designed websites which pollute the cyber world." Professor Tom Costa of the University of Virginia and his team are therefore much to be congratulated upon his achievement in bringing to the Internet the most versatile index to eighteenth-century newspaper advertisements for runaways yet produced.

Maryland Runaway Servants

The search for runaways in Maryland from 1728 to 1775 has been dramatically simplified by the provision through the Maryland State Archives of detailed indexes to runaway advertisements carried in the *Maryland Gazette* from 1728 to 1775. They are to be found online at www2.vcdh.virginia.edu.gos/search/seach.php and photocopies of the original texts may be ordered at very reasonable cost.

The data obtained in this way has then been checked against British judicial and other records of trials and sentences and any further relevant information added to the following lists. It will be appreciated that this procedure is bound to present some severe difficulties. The criminal fraternity not only adopted a variety of familiar alternative names (Smith, Jones, Robinson and Evans were popular choices) but even their preferred nomenclature, once it had been processed through the hands of officials and newspaper editors, was liable to take a distorted format.

Virginia Runaway Servants

The internet address given above will make accessible the pages of Professor Costa's listings from the *Virginia Gazette* and show clearly the gaps in publication between 1729 and 1745, after which issues become more regular.

Peter Wilson Coldham
October 2011, AMDG

Runaway Servants from Maryland and Virginia

Abbott, John, no age stated, Runaway Irish Convict Servant, tall, stout with his left arm marked I.A in Indian ink, imported in the *Justitia* for life from London Sessions. From John Strother of Culpeper Co, VA. (VG 26 Jan 1769).

Able, Thomas, about 25, Runaway English Servant [sentenced to transportation at Middlesex Sessions and landed from the *Thornton* in Anne Arundel Co, VA, in Jul 1771) having a red face and very rotten teeth, a great talker pitted with smallpox. From William Smithson living near Bush River, Harford Co, MD. (VG 21 Apr 1775).

Ablewhite, Thomas, no age given, Runaway Servant. From Thomas Nevett of Cambridge, Great Choptank River, MD. (VG 15-22 Oct 1736).

Acland, John, no age stated, Runaway Servant, short and well set, by trade a tailor, supposed to have gone towards Carolina. From John Bland at Blandford, VA. (VG 27 Apr 1769); from Margaret Harper in Petersburg, VA. (VG 24 May 1770).

Adams, Britain, about 13, Apprentice of yellow complexion and very thin made. From Thomas Llewellin, Williamsburg, VA. (VG 19 Mar 1772).

Adams, James, no age given, Runaway Sailor from ship *Theodorick* lying at Broadway, Appamatox; he speaks broad inclining to a Yorkshire accent. From Hugh Wylie of said ship. (VG 8 Feb 1770).

Adams, James, about 23, Suspected Runaway English Servant who says he was born in England and his master is Jeremiah Alderson of Prince Edward Co., VA. Owner to contact John Cawley, Gaoler of Augusta Co,. VA, Gaol. (VG 30 Sep 1773).

Adams, William. Suspected Runaway, 15 or 19, says he is a Convict Servant, weaver belonging to William Bartlett (Barkley) of Loudoun Co, VA, talks broad Scotch. *Probably the youth of that name transported from Kent Assizes for 14 years by the ship* Thornton *to MD in 1768.* Claimed by William Barkley 27 Sep 1770; committed to Goochland Co Gaol, VA, by Robert Coleman. (VG 4 Oct 1770).

Aiken, David, about 35, Runaway Scotsman with slight smallpox who deserted the vessel *Molly* on Hampton River, VA, and supposedly gone towards MD. From James Graham of Hampton.(VG 6 Oct 1752).

Aldred, Giles, about 25, Runaway Convict Servant with red hair and a mark where his right arm was broken, a weaver with a Welsh accent, [*transported from Lancashire Quarter Sessions in Oct 1771*]. From John Leitch, Prince Edward Co, VA. (VG 18 Mar 1773.

Alexander, William, no age given, Runaway English Convict Servant, much pitted with smallpox, wears a sober face and talks little. [*Transported from London Sessions by the* Justitia *in 1767*]. From Robert Phillips at Fredericksburg, VA. (VG 28 Jan 1768).

Alford, Drury, no age given, of Albemarle Co, VA, Runaway Deserter Recruit raised for the Georgia Service. From Robert & George Walton at Prince Edward Courthouse, VA. (VG 27 Sep 1776).

Allay, Barnaby, about 50, Runaway Irish Convict Servant who speaks tolerably good English and pretends to understand the sailor's business; he walks almost on his knees when drinking. From John Quarles Jr of King William Co Courthouse, VA. (VG 7 Nov 1754).

Allen, George, about 25, Runaway English Convict Servant [sentenced at Middlesex Sessions in 1773 to be transported by the Tayloe but taken from that ship for his case and that of his brother John Allen to be reviewed], lately imported by the Justitia consigned to Thomas Hodge at Leeds Town, VA. He is remarkably round-shouldered and stoops much. From Thomas Montgomerie, Dumfries, VA. (VG 12 May 1774).

Allen, James, Runaway Servant committed to Loudoun Co Gaol who says he belongs to James Brown of Culpeper Co Gaol. Owner to apply to gaoler John Herriford. (VG 5 Sep 1771).

Allen, John, no age given, Runaway Mulatto Servant, tall and slim, by trade a shoemaker. From John Muirhead at Norfolk, VA. (VG 23 Nov 1769).

Allen, John, no age given, Runaway English Convict Servant, brother of George Allen (q.v.), slender made. [sentenced at Middlesex Sessions in 1773 to be transported by the Tayloe but taken from that ship for his case and that of his brother George Allen to be reviewed], lately imported by the Justitia consigned to Thomas Hodge at Leeds Town, VA. From Thomas Montgomerie, Dumfries, VA. (VG 12 May 1774).

Allen, Matthew, no age given, Runaway Apprentice Lad so well known in New Kent C, VA, that a description is needless. From Thomas Pate, Williamsburg, VA. (VG 10 Feb 1776).

Allinsord, Philip. *See* Helensord.

Almond, John, no age given, Runaway English Servant who deserted the ship *Allerton* lying at Berkeley, James River, VA. From James Wallace of the said vessel. (VG 21 Aug 1752).

Amens alias Emens, Joseph, no age stated, Runaway Sailor who left his shipmates who were imported in the *Queensborough* in 1750 and lurking about Williamsborough, VA. From Hannah Critendon near the brickhouse, New Kent Co, VA. (VG 25 Apr 1751).

Anderson, Bartlett, no age given, Runaway Soldier Deserter, a very tall waggoner from 2nd Battalion recruited in VA for defence of GA but who rode off in Prince Edward Co. From Lieut John Clarke, Cumberland Co, VA. (VG 7 Mar 1777).

Anderson, Richard, no age given, Deserter from Capt Reuben Lipscomb's Co in Amelia Co, VA. Reward offered by Lieut Tarpley White, Williamsburg, VA. (VG 28 Mar 1777).

Arbado, Francis, about 30, a black Frenchman, Runaway Seaman Deserter from the galley *Manly*. From William Saunders of said vessel, Williamsburg, VA. (VG 16 May 1777).

Archer, Lawford, about 20, Runaway Servant much pox-ridden and has large legs, has been employed for 3-4 years as a store boy. From Nathaniel Chapman, Accokeek Mines, Stafford Co, VA. (VG 10-17 Feb 1738).

Armstrong, William, 27, Scottish Convict Servant, blacksmith. From John Augustine Washington or John Turberville, Westmoreland Co, VA. (VG 26 Jul 1775).

Arter, William, no age given, Runaway Apprentice Servant, carpenter. From Francis Smith Sr of King William Co, VA, Courthouse. (VG 2 Apr 1767).

Ashbill, David, about 35, Irish Runaway Servant, professed farmer with a fierce countenance and a thin and pox-ridden face. From Robert Vaulx of Westmoreland, Co, Potomac , VA. (VG 2 May 1751).

Atkinson, Philip, 30, Deserted from Pittsylvania Regular Company in Williamsburg. From Capt Thomas Hutchings, Headquarters, Williamsburg, VA. (VG 24 May 1776).

Ausler, Jeremiah, about 18, Convict Servant. From ship *Duke of Cumberland* at Bermuda Hundred, James River, VA. From Joseph Barnes, master of said ship. (VG 18-25 May 1739).

Avery (Evrie/Everee), John, about 29, Scotch Convict Servant [*transported from Middlesex Sessions by the Justitia in 1767, weaver*] cunning and artful, recently flogged. From N.N. Dandridge, Hanover Co, VA. (VG 18 Jan 24 May 1770).

Axley, James, no age given, Runaway Apprentice Servant, carpenter [*one of this name transported from Surrey Assizes in Sep 1730 to VA by the ship* Smith]. From Francis Smith Sr of King William Co, VA, Courthouse , (VG 2 Apr 1767).

Bachelor (Batchelor), Peter, about 23, [son of Paul Batchelor, sentenced to transportation at Middlesex Sessions for stealing a watch and shipped to MD in Jul 1770 by the ship *Scarsdale*]. Runaway English Convict Servant. From Joseph Strother near Thornton's Pass in Culpeper, VA. (VG 4 Jul 1771).

Bagnall, John, about 20, Convict Servant [*? Transported from Nottingham Assizes in 1771*) imported in November 1772 in the *Alexandria* and bought at Leeds Town on Rappahannock River, Va: he was born in London, served his apprenticeship as a tinplate worker and was carried off by Convict Servant William Harris, bricklayer belonging to Capt Joseph Pierce of Westmoreland, VA. From Roger Beckwith near Rappahannock Bridge, Richmond Co, VA. (VG 30 Jul 1772).

Baillie, Stephen, about 16, well grown Servant boy. From Archibald McCaul of Essex Co, VA. (VG 12 Dec 1755.

Bailey, Anne, about 30 [*probably sentenced at London Sessions for stealing at Blackfriars and transported to VA in Feb 1769 by the* Thornton]. Suspected Runaway who says she belongs to John Orm of George Town, MD. The owner to take her away and pay charges. From B. Johnston, gaoler of Spotsylvania Co, VA. (VG 20 Jun 1771).

Bailey, Daniel, no age given, Runaway Soldier Deserter from 2nd Battalion for Georgia. From Joseph Pannill, Prince Edward Courthouse, VA. (VG 27 Dec 1776).

Bailey, Josiah, 25, Runaway English Servant with a scar on his chest caused by a scald, hangs his head when he walks and takes short steps, a leather breeches maker. From William Blyth, Fredericksburg, VA. (VG 21 Sep 1775).

Bailey, Samuel, 24-30, Runaway Convict Servant who has been about two years in the country [*probably transported by the* Justitia *in Dec 1769 from London Sessions*]; has a much swollen and sore leg, and a remarkably grey head caused by smallpox, by trade a house joiner. From William Buckland of Richmond Co, VA. (VG 26 Jul & 1 Aug 1771).

Bain, John, about 24, Runaway English Servant with a face full of spots and pimples who is much addicted to liquor and supposedly intended for Alexandria, by trade a tailor. From Robert Nicolson, Williamsburg, VA. (VG 19 Aug 1773).

Baker, Mary, no age given, Runaway Servant [*probably transported from Devonshire Assizes in 1768*], who speaks very bad English. From Thomas Green near the Sugar Lands, Frederick Co, MD.(VG 21 Sep 1769).

Baker, Richard, no age given [possibly the one of that name convicted at the London Sessions for stealing a hat in Feb and transported to MD in Apr 1768 by the *Thornton*]. Runaway Convict Servant, very talkative and will deceive anyone with his tongue, the driver of a dray. From John Reed, Baltimore, MD.(VG 6 Feb 1772).

Balding, William, 22-23, Runaway Indented English Servant, small in size, who ran from plantation of James Pride, by trade a carpenter and joiner. From William Chancey of Williamsburg, VA. (VG 18 Aug 1774).

Ball, Susanna, no age given, Runaway Convict Servant imported in December 1773 in the *Success's Increase*, small woman with disagreeable temper, ran from Forceput six miles from Fredericksburg, VA. From H Grymes of Forceput. (VG 7 Apr 1774).

Barber, James, about 25, Runaway English Convict Servant [*transported from Lent 1770 Nottingham Assizes*]. From Benjamin Howard near Elk Ridge Landing, VA. (VG 18 Jul 1771).

Barber, W., no age given, Runaway Servant, a West Country fellow who talks broad, has a dark mothy complexion and a scar on his forehead. From Daniel Hornby, Williamsburg, VA. (VG 26 Aug-2 Sep 1737).

Barns, Gerard, about 40, Runaway Convict Servant, much scarred on the head and nose and has a down look; he stole his indentures. From Ephraim Furr near Levin Powel's store in Loudoun Co, VA. (VG 18 Oct 1770).

Barnes, Mary, no age given, [*sentenced at London Sessions in May 1736 and transported to MD the same month by the* Patapsco Merchant], has a sickly countenance and is much bloated. From Thomas Nevett of Cambridge, Great Choptank River, MD. (VG 15-22 Oct 1736).

Barnett, David, 21, 6 feet 4 inches tall, thin face caused by ague and fever incurred when he deserted; he speaks but seldom, Runaway Deserter at Deep Spring Camp, Williamsburg, from a company of rifleman of 6th Virginia Regiment at New York. From Capt Samuel Jordan Cabell of said Regiment. (VG 8 Nov 1776).

Barnett, James, Deserter from Camp at Maidstone, VA, born in MD. From Commanding Officer, Winchester, VA. (VG 27 Aug 1756).

Barret, Anne, about 24, Runaway English Convict pitted with smallpox and with a small nose. (?*transported from London Assizes by the* Lichfield *in* 1748). From Willoughby Newton of

Westmoreland Co, VA. (VG 5 Mar 1752).

Barry, George, 16-17, Convict Lad, barber by trade. Runaway Servant. From John Lewis of Gloucester Co, VA. (VG 21-28 Apr 1738).

Barry, Ned, 50-60, Runaway Servant (*possibly the Edward Barry sentenced at Middlesex Sessions and transported for 14 years by the* Tayloe *in Jul 1772*), bald headed who has much of the brogue. From James Crow near Staunton, Augusta Co, VA. (VG 7 Jun 1776).

Bartholomew, John, about 26, English Servant, tailor. From Robert Hutchings, Petersburg,VA. (VG 7 Nov 1751).

Bartlett, James, 24, born in London, a thin spare lad, Runaway Seaman who deserted the sloop of war *American Congress* in Yeocomico, Northumberland Co, VA. From John Allison, Capt of Marines of said vessel. (VG 21 Jun 1776).

Barton, Elias, no age given, Runaway Servant who stoops in his walk, treads uncommonly hard, seldom looks anyone in the face when talking and stammers a little; he is marked with smallpox. From Peter Hoffman and Abraham Faw of Frederick Town, MD. (VG 10 Nov 1774).

Basten, Edward, middle-aged, Runaway Convict Servant with a stooped walk and bald head. From Robert Jackson of Fredericksburg, VA. (VG 8 Aug 1751).

Bate, John, about 23, Runaway English Convict Servant. From Benjamin Howard near Elk Ridge Landing, VA. (VG 18 Jun 1771).

Bates, John, 27-28, stout and well looking Runaway English Convict Servant. From Benjamin Howard near Elk Ridge Landing, VA. (VG 18 Jun 1771).

Beaver, Elizabeth, about 20, Servant Runaway with short hair uncommonly cut who ran off without hat or bonnet with a mulatto slave named Sancho aged about 40 and will probably pass for husband and wife. From Joseph Calland of Cumberland Co, VA. (VG 17 Mar 1774).

Beckly, William, no age given, Runaway Seaman of the ship *London* lying before Yorktown, VA. From Moses Robertson of said ship. (VG 16 Jun 1774).

Belcher, Thomas, about 28, Runaway English Convict Servant imported into Patapsco River, MD, in July 1765, well made and speaks effeminately; his occupation is farming and he pretends to knowledge in many other kinds of business. From Joseph Watkins of New Kent Co, VA. (VG 16 Mar 1769).

Bell, James, Runaway Convict Servant, no age stated, about 6 feet 11 inches tall, red complexion, painter by trade. From John Champe, Williamsburg, VA. (VG 11 May 1769).

Bell, James, about 40, Runaway Indented Servant, a miner from Yorkshire. From Samuel Hanson, Charles Co, MD. (VG 24 Nov 1774).

Bellaman, William, no age given, Runaway Servant somewhat pox-ridden. From Cornelius Sale of Essex Co, VA. (VG 13-20 Oct 1738).

Belong, Joseph, 35, Runaway Convict Servant from the West of England, a joiner. From George Steuart, Williamsburg, VA. (VG 7 Jul 1774).

Belvin, Aaron, no age given, Runaway Soldier Deserter from Capt Charles Tomkies' Co of 7th Regiment and probably now in Gloucester Co, VA, where it was raised. From Reuben Lipscomb, Williamsburg, VA. (VG 24 Jan 1777).

Belvin, George, no age given, Runaway Soldier Deserter from Capt Charles Tomkies' Co of 7th Regiment and probably now in Gloucester Co, VA, where it was raised. From Reuben Lipscomb, Williamsburg, VA. (VG 24 Jan 1777).

Belvin, Lewis, no age given, Runaway Soldier Deserter from Capt Charles Tomkies' Co of 7th Regiment and probably now in Gloucester Co, VA, where it was raised. From Reuben Lipscomb, Williamsburg, VA. (VG 24 Jan 1777).

Bemish, Thomas, Runaway English Indented Servant, no age stated, scar on his chest the size of a dollar and scar on his right leg caused by an axe; he was sold as a bricklayer but knows nothing of the business. From Daniel Lipscombe, King William Co Courthouse. (VG 15 Sep 1775).

Benfield, Sarah, about 30, Runaway English Servant with bad teeth who speaks a very broad Lancashire dialect. From John Stretch of Williamsburg, VA. (VG 29 Sep 1752).

Benham (Benhan), John, about 28, Runaway English Convict Servant with stooped shoulders and hoarse voice, blacksmith by trade, (*transported from Middlesex Sessions by the* Justitia *in 1767*). From William Carr Lane near Rocky Run Chapel, Loudoun Co, VA. (VG 12 May 1768).

Bennett, George, Runaway English Soldier from camp at Williamsburg, VA, about 19, robbed a store on James River. From William Gooch at Williamsburg Camp. (VG 24-31 Jul 1746).

Bennett, Richard, about 18, Convict Servant Runaway, jobbing blacksmith, pert and sly. Transported from London by *Justitia* and supposedly gone to NC. From Sampson & George Matthews of Richmond, VA. (VG 12 Aug 1773).

Benson, Thomas, no age given, Runaway Irish Servant who has lost half his left little finger, a good scholar. From Nathaniel Morgan, Fincastle, VA. (VG 30 Jun 1775).

Bentley, Thomas, no age given, Indented Servant bound for 4 years in England, about 6 feet tall, impudent talker, coachman. From Philip Ludwell Lee, Stratford, VA. (VG 16 & 23 Aug 1770).

Bern, Richard, no age given, Runaway Servant with a scar over his right eye, a tailor by trade. From William Lightfoot of Teddington, ?VA. (VG 22 Jan 1752).

Berry, John, no age given, Irish Runaway Convict with very much brogue. From James Toone of Richmond Co, VA. (VG 15-22 Sep 1738).

Berry, Elizabeth, no age given, Runaway English Convict Servant (transported as Elizabeth Berry, wife of Richard, alias Elizabeth Wade of Manchester from Lancaster Quarter Sessions in 1768),

Berry, John, about 30, Runaway Swedish Sailor who ran from the *Maryland Merchant* lying at York Town, VA. From Stephen Jerman Jr of said ship. (VG 22-29 May 1746).

Bevan, Thomas, about 25, Runaway English Servant who came from London in May 1770 by the *Vulture*, Capt Thomas Jordan, a button maker by trade and pitted with smallpox. From James Miller of Bladensburg, MD.(VG 17 Jan 1771).

Beveridge, Henry Valentine, about 28, Runaway English Convict, skinner or tanner by trade, transported hither by the *Dorsetshire*, Capt Bowman in July 1745.From Samuel Hilldrup of Fredericksburg, VA. (VG 17-24 Apr 1746).

Biggs, Randolph, 19, born in Fairfax Co, VA, Runaway Seaman who deserted the sloop of war *American Congress* in Yeocomico, Northumberland Co, VA. From John Allison, Capt of Marines of said vessel. (VG 21 Jun 1776).

Bilbery, Nathaniel, about 20, of Edgecombe Co, NC, Runaway Soldier Deserter from 3rd Regiment of NC Continental Troops. From Capt James Bradby. (VG 9 May 1777).

Billingham, Edward, about 30, Convict chimney sweeper & labourer born in north of England & speaks like a Scotsman. From Sampson Matthews of Staunton, Augusta Co, VA. (VG 17 Oct 1766).

Bird, Robert, about 22, Runaway English Servant, shoemaker by trade. From Anthony Lynton of Acquia, Stafford Co, VA. (VG 14-21 Jul 1738).

Bissey, John, about 20, who has a bold saucy look and is much pitted with smallpox. From Edward Stevenson, Little Pipe Creek, Frederick Co, MD. (VG 12 Mar 1772).

Blackburn, George, about 22, Runaway Indented English Servant born in Co Durham, with remarkably long fingers, pretty well learned with a good hand and is carefully dressed; he is a sensible obliging man. From Thomas & Samuel Pretlow, Williamsburg, VA. (VG 29 Apr 1775).

Blackburn, Robert, 24, Lieut Col Burton's Co in Col Dunbar's Regiment who served his time as a labourer with William Webb JP at Little Land Tatem in MD. From General Braddock at Winchester, VA. (VG 9 May 1755).

Blacknall, Thomas, no age given, Runaway Soldier Deserter from Capt Charles Tomkies' Co of 7th Regiment and probably now in Gloucester Co, VA, where it was raised. From Reuben Lipscomb, Williamsburg, VA. (VG 24 Jan 1777).

Blair, Joseph Mitchell, about 23, Runaway Deserter from Halifax Regular Co now in Williamsburg. From Capt Nathaniel Cocke. (VG 20 Apr & 10 May 1776).

Blanchlet, William, about 27, thin face, sharp nose and black beard. From Thomas Saunders living near Bush River, Harford Co, MD.(VG 21 Apr 1775).

Blashford, Michael, no age given, Irish Servant. From Richard Arell of Alexandria, VA. (VG 23 May 1771).

Blasingham (Blasingame), Benjamin Hope, about 17, Runaway Apprentice tailor of middle size with a down look who has served three years in the business. From Henry Hall, near Courthouse of Gloucester Co, VA. (VG 7 & 14 Jan 1773).

Blathyn, William, no age stated, Runaway Welsh Servant, small and sprightly, house carpenter and joiner, supposed to be heading for Carolina. From Harry Gaines from estate of William Byrd at Westover, VA. (VG 27 Mar 1752).

Bohannon, Joseph, no age given, Suspected Deserter from Deep Spring Camp, VA, of 6th Virginia Regiment. Warning from Capt James Johnson of said Regt. (VG 30 Aug 1776).

Bolton, William, 19, Runaway Apprentice Boy, clumsy made with a very fair countenance, apt to swear and lie, who ran from divine service and has run once before. From James Gardener, carpenter of Williamsburg, VA. (VG 18 Mar & 19 Aug 1773).

Booker, John, about 31, Runaway English Convict of Waddington, Yorks, (*transported from Yorkshire Quarter Sessions in Jan 1770*) imported in the *Nassau*, Capt Wignall, just arrived in Rappahannock from Liverpool; he has a ruddy countenance, a down look and is little marked by smallpox, fond of liquor and talkative, a good ditcher. From James Duncanson, Fredericksburg, VA. (VG 21 Jun & 12 Jul 1770); he ran (aged 33) from the same master in Apr 1772. (VG 23 Apr 1772). But see advertisement of 8 Oct 1772 for William Watson (q.v.) aged 38 in Westmoreland Co Gaol.

Booth, Charles, 20-21, Runaway English Indented Servant, by trade a joiner. From William Brent in Stafford Co, VA. (VG 5 & 7 Jan 1775).

Boothman, Jonathan, 23, Runaway English Convict Servant (*Transported from Middlesex Sessions in 1773*) who ran from the *Tayloe* at Four Mile Creek, VA. He has a thievish look. From Sampson & George Mathews, Williamsburg, VA. (VG 11 Nov 1773).

Bostock, John, about 21, Suspected Runaway English Servant who has lost the second joint of the little finger of his right hand. From William Lane, gaoler ?of Williamsburg, VA. (VG 11 Oct 1770).

Boughan, Francis, about 20, born in Essex. Deserter from Capt Thomas Waggoner's Co at Fredericksburg, VA. From Henry Woodward at Fredericksburg. (VG 28 Feb 1755).

Bourk, William, no age given, Runaway Irish Servant, short and well made, much pitted with smallpox, sawyer by trade. From LeRoy Griffin of Richmond Co, VA. (VG 13-20 May 1737).

Boyce, Thomas, 30-40, Runaway English Servant much pitted with smallpox. From William Settle, near the Fauquier Co Courthouse, VA. (VG 4 Aug 1774).

Boyd, John, about 30, Runaway Deserter Soldier with some scars about his mouth who says he was born in New England and is a shoemaker by trade; he deserted from the College Camp, Williamsburg. From Francis Taylor, Williamsburg. (VG 6 Sep 1776).

Bradburn, Francis, 23, Deserter from Camp at Maidstone, VA, born in MD. From Commanding Officer, Winchester, VA. (VG 27 Aug 1756).

Bragg, William, about 40, stout and when drunk talkative and impertinent, formerly an inhabitant of Culpeper living near Bradley's ordinary, Runaway Deserter from Capt Spender's Co of Regulars before they left Orange Co. From Joseph Spencer, Williamsburg Headquarters. (VG 5 Jul 1776).

Brannan, Timothy, no age given, Runaway Irish Servant committed to Augusta Co Gaol who says he belongs to John Lynn near Sleepy Run church, Prince William Co, VA. The owner to apply to George Matthews, Sheriff of Augusta. (VG 17 Oct 1771).

Brasenton, William, 18-19, Runaway Apprentice Boy with a wen over his left eye and a mark on his left forefinger caused by a needle used when he was learning the tailor business. From George Collins, Portsmouth, VA. (VG 22 Oct 1772).

Brenon, James alias O'Brian, John, no age given, Runaway Indented Irish Servant born in Dublin, slender arms and body, tailor by trade, can write very well. From William Davis of York Town, VA. (VG 24, 29 & 30 Jun 1775).

Brewster, John, about 25, Runaway Servant, blacksmith by trade who ran away 18 months ago and was taken. From [unstated] of Rock Creek, Frederick Co, MD. (VG 10 Apr 1752).

Brimhead, William, no age given, Runaway English Servant Boy, slender and poxridden who stammers, shoemaker by trade, supposed to be gone to Augusta, VA. From Matthew Willman of Hanover Co. (VG 7 Nov 1755).

Britt, John, 26, Runaway Irish Marine Deserter, stout, much pitted with smallpox, a blemished eye and suffering from venereal disease. From Samuel Arell, Alexandria, VA. (VG 27 Dec 1776).

Brown, James, no age given, Deserter from Lieut John Hall at Suffolk, VA, very stupid appearance, addicted to liquor. (VG 3 Oct 1755).

Brown, John, about 24, Runaway Scotsman born in Leith who deserted froe ship *Berry*. From James Belcher at Sheppard's Warehouse, Williamsburg, VA. (VG 27 Mar 1752).

Brown, John, about 35, Runaway English Servant with large temples, narrow chin and thick lips who is used to the sea. From Buckler Bond living near Bush River, Harford Co, MD. (VG 21 Apr 1775).

Brown, William alias Danally (Donally), William, Runaway Irish Servant marked with the letter W. on one hand. From Mrs Bordland of Hampton, VA. (VG 9-16 Sep 1737).

Brown, William, no age given, blacksmith by trade, Runaway Servant of Richard Adams. From George Donald of Richmond Town, VA. (VG 7 Mar 1766).

Browning, Christopher, about 24, Runaway English Servant who has been a Marine and is subject to fits; he pretends to understand butchery and was imported in the *Becky*. From William Freeman of Norfolk Borough, VA. (VG 10 Jan 1752).

Browning, George Jr, no age given, Runaway English Convict Servant (*sentenced in Apr 1774 to be transported for life from Gloucestershire Assizes for murder*). He was born in Bristol, England, is lame in one knee and walks with a stick; he can write with a blotched hand; by trade a shoemaker. From Christopher Curtis, Henrico Co, VA. (VG 24 Nov 1774).

Bruce, James, about 26, Runaway Indented Shoemaker pitted with smallpox. From William Forsyth & Co, Portsmouth, VA. (VG 5 Mar 1772).

Bruce, James, 25, Runaway Indented Scottish Seaman. From William Black in King and Queen Co, VA. (VG 9 Jul 1772).

Bruce, John, about 24, Runaway Sailor from the ship *Vernon* at Hampton, VA. From Anthony Langton of the said ship. (VG 7-14 Aug 1746).

Bruton, John, no age given, Runaway Servant, full faced, bow-legged, a scar on his thumb. From William Withers in Fauquier Co, VA. (VG 10 Mar 1775).

Bryan, Edward, 30, Runaway Irish Servant much pitted with smallpox, near sighted and unpromising countenance. From John Dalton of Alexandria, VA. (VG 23 Jul 1767).

Bryant, Joseph, no age given, Runaway Soldier Deserter from 2nd Virginia Regiment in NJ, enlisted in King George Co, VA, where his parents live, fond of liquor with a remarkable scar on one lip. From Col Alexander Spotswood of said Regiment. (VG 5 Sep 1777).

Bulger, John, about 17, Runaway English Convict Servant, pitted with smallpox; transported from Middlesex, England, by the *Justitia* in 1768. From Anthony Thornton Jr at Recovery furnace, Spotsylvania Co, VA. (VG 21 Jun 1770).

Bulling, Richard, an old man and very grey (*transported from Essex Assizes by the Dorsetshire in 1738*). From John Johnston, Courthouse, Westmoreland Co, VA. (VG 16-23 Feb 1738).

Bullock, James, no age given, Runaway Servant who enlisted with an officer Robert Poythress of the Georgia service who refused to return him. From James Anderson of Prince George Co, VA. (VG 6 Dec 1776).

Bullock, Thomas, about 27, Runaway Englishman who ran from the *Industrious Bee* at Sandy Point, VA. From Henry Pascal of the said vessel. (VG 5 Jun 1752).

Bunkley, John, about 30, Indentured Servant, dark and sunburnt, has lost his left leg below the knee and has wooden one. From Luke Sumner of Chowan Co, NC. (VG 14 Apr 1758).

Bunn, Arthur, about 30, Runaway English Servant. From Robert Wallace of Walker's Creek, Augusta, VA. (VG 10 Jun 1773).

Burk, Patrick, about 30, born in VA, saddler. From James Mitchell, York Town, VA. (VG 4-11 Mar 1737).

Burks, James, 19-20, Runaway Irish Convict Servant who speaks much on the brogue and burnt the advertiser's house. From John Mason near the head of Great Nottoway, Lunenburg Co, VA. (VG 1 Jun 1779).

Burn, Francis, about 22, Convict Servant. From William Kelly of Orange Co, VA. (VG 17-24 Apr 1746).

Burn, James, no age given, Suspected Runaway Irish Servant much pitted with smallpox and carrying papers belonging to Mr Holebreech of MD. Owner to apply to Thomas Clifton, gaoler of Culpeper Prison. (VG 22 Mar 1770).

Burn, Michael, no age given, Servant. From James Crop Jr of Potomack, VA. (VG 3 Nov 1752).

Burn, Philip, born about 1702, Irish Convict Servant. From Harry Gaines, King William Co, VA. (VG, 18 Jun 1752).

Burnett (Barnet) alias Cole, William, no age given, Runaway English Convict sentenced to transportation at Berkshire Assizes in 1736 for highway robbery. From James Boyd of Fredericksburg, Spotsylvania Co, VA. (VG 2-9 Mar 1739).

Burrage, John, no age given, Runaway Indentured Servant much marked with smallpox, a clock and watch marker. From Frances Knapp of Williamsburg, VA. (VG 3 Aug 1769).

Bush, Charles, born 4 May 1749, bastard. From Richard Quinn, Culpeper Co, VA. (VG 12 May 1768).

Butler, Charles, no age given, Runaway English Indented Servant with very black hair and a remarkable black beard, by trade a saddler and harness maker. From Miles Taylor, Richmond Town, Henrico Co, VA. (VG 28 Apr 1774).

Butler, Edmund, about 15, Runaway Irish Servant, born in Cork. From Benjamin Catton of York Town, VA. (VG 20-27 Mar 1746).

Butler, Edward, about 27, [*transported from Middlesex Sessions by the* Tayloe *in Jul 1773*], Runaway English Convict Servant,, lusty and well-set, by trade a tailor. From Benjamin Colvard and George Divers in Albemarle, VA. (VG 21 Jul 1774).

Butler, James, no age given, Suspected Deserter from Deep Spring Camp, VA, of 6th Virginia Regiment. Warning from Capt James Johnson of said Regt. (VG 30 Aug 1776).

Butler, John (1739) – *See* Collins, John.

Butler, Peter, about 24, Runaway English Servant much pitted with smallpox, pretends to be a butcher by trade; he was brought in aboard the *Baltimore*, Capt Robinson, at West Point in King William Co, VA, and ran the same day. From David Stewart near the Courthouse in Augusta Co, VA. (VG 11 Jul 1751).

Butler, Thomas, alias Richard How, about 25, [*Thomas Griffis alias Butler transported from Middlesex Assizes by the* Duke of Cumberland *in 1739*], Runaway English Convict, by trade a plasterer, pale and pox-marked face, last seen in Norfolk, VA, and believed to be concealed with a lame shoemaker and a woman of evil fame. (VG 16-23 May 1745).

Cagan, Brian, about 50, Runaway Irish Servant who pretends to be a miller and millwright. From Richard Barnes of Richmond Co, VA. (VG 2-9 Jun 1738).

Caine, John, no age given, Runaway Soldier Deserter from 2nd Georgia Battalion who enlisted in Williamsburg, VA. From Lieut Robert Ward, Williamsburg. (VG 24 Jan 1777).

Caldwell, David, about 24, Runaway Scottish Sailor, thin, short and fat, who speaks broad Scotch and left the *Prince William*, on Pamunkey River. From Capt William Smith of the said ship. (VG 18 Apr 1751).

Calvert, John, no age given, Runaway Seaman Deserter from the sloop *Scorpion* who speaks the North Country dialect. From Wright Westcott of said vessel. (VG 4 Oct 1776).

Campbell, Hugh, about 18, Runaway Apprentice who was born at sea and cannot read or write; he came from Albemarle Co and will probably go that way. From John Richardson of York Town, VA. (VG 14 Aug 1752).

Cambell (alias Mitchell), James, about 26, [*sentenced at Cumberland Sessions in 1736 for stealing a horse at Summer Session 1736 & transported to VA in Summer 1737*], tall Scottish Servant. From Benjamin Berryman of King George Co, VA. (VG 23-30 Mar 1739).

Campbell, John, no age stated, Irishman of no trade, short, broad and fat. From John Mitchell of Urbanna, VA. (VG 16-23 Mar 1739).

Campbell, John, about 30, Irish born Convict Servant, both legs cut, runaway from Marlborough Forge, Frederick Co, VA. From William Holmes. (VG 3 Jan 1771).

Campbell, John, no age given, Deserter from Capt John Blair's Co of 9th Virginia Regiment when under marching orders. From Lieut Thomas Overton, Williamsburg, VA. (VG 11 Jul 1777).

Campion, German, 30, indented servant born in Derbyshire, England. From John Augustine Washington or John Turberville, Westmoreland Co, VA. (VG 26 Jul 1775).

Canterbury, Joseph, 28, has short red hair and a dejected look; he was enlisted in Amherst. Runaway Deserter at Deep Spring Camp, Williamsburg, from a company of rifleman of 6th Virginia Regiment at New York. From Capt Samuel Jordan Cabell of said Regiment. (VG 8 Nov 1776).

Cantwell, Edward, no age given, Runaway Soldier Deserter from 2nd Battalion for Georgia. From Joseph Pannill, Prince Edward Courthouse, VA. (VG 27 Dec 1776).

Cantwell, William, 19, Runaway English Servant born in Warwickshire, somewhat marked with smallpox, pretends to understand ploughing and country business and has driven a wagon in service. From John Mercer of Marlborough, Stafford Co, VA. (VG 6 Jun 1766).

Carey, James, about 17, Runaway who was given £13 to release him from being sent to MD and sold, and to be bound as an apprentice; he is stout made and as a native of Ireland speaks thick and on the brogue. From Purdie & Dixon, Williamsburg, VA. (VG 24 Jan 1771).

Carlile, Anne, about 20, Runaway Indentured Servant who has a scar on her forehead, a pretended mantua maker who is supposed to have gone down to Norfolk, VA. From John Brittan near Osborne's in Chesterfield, VA. (VG 24 Mar 1768).

Carnes, Arundell, about 17, Convict Servant imported by the *Tryal* in April 1766 [*in Middlesex Quarter Sessions table in transportation listings but not in other English records*], he pretends to be something of a doctor, will probably make for MD. From Thomas Lawson, Neabsco furnace, Prince William Co, Va.(VG 29 Aug 1766).

Carney, Bartholomew, about 35, Runaway Servant with a very short nose and pitted with smallpox. From Jeremiah Owen of Fauquier Co, VA. (VG 11 Oct 1770).

Carpenter, Joseph, about 26, Runaway English Servant, fat and thick, can write very well and pretends to be a coppersmith and brazier. From William Lynn in Fredericksburg, VA. (VG 30 Jul 1752).

Carpenter, Timothy, no age given, [*sentenced to be transported for 14 years Berkshire Assizes in Summer 1756*], Runaway Convict Servant who is young and slim and has the marks of the irons he wore on his ankles in gaol. He was imported in 1756 by the *Hodgson*, Capt Pajer, and ran away from the schooner *Billy* at Hobb's Hole, VA. From Hon John Tayloe of the Ironworks in Prince William Co, VA. (VG 2 Sep 1757).

Carrick, Patrick, no age given, Irish Runaway Deserter, talks hoarse and in the brogue, much pitted with smallpox, shipped from 8th Regiment as seaman in cruiser *Revenge*, Capt William Deane. Runaway from Aaron Jeffery, Cumberland Co, VA. (VG 19 Jul 1776).

Carrell, Dugless, no age given, Runaway Soldier Deserter from 3rd Regiment of NC enlisted in Bute Co, NC, slender with reddish hair. From Lieut William Linton. (VG 9 May 1777).

Carroll, Patrick, about 28, Irish Convict Servant, handy as planter, ditcher or gardener. From John Martin, Attorney at Law of King William Co, VA. (VG 30 May – 6 Jun 1745 & 22-29 May 1746).

Carroll, Sarah, no age given, tall, slender and swarthy, weaver by trade, runaway with Patrick Flodd (q.v.) and seen on the road to Carolina. From John Mitchell of Urbanna, Middlesex Co, VA. (VG 10-17 Mar 1738).

Carroll, William, about 30, Suspected Runaway Servant committed to Winchester Gaol in Frederick Co, VA; he denies he is a servant and that Matthias Merritt of Surry Co will testify he is a freeman. Application to be made to gaoler John Lyne. (VG 13 Sep 1770).

Carry, John, no age given, Runaway Irish Servant, reputed blacksmith, a great rogue to whom a whipping will be of great service. From William Aylett of Essex Co, VA. (VG 30 Mar-6 Apr 1739).

Carter alias Gasford, Samuel, about 23, [transported *for life from Middlesex Sessions* by the Thornton *to Rappahannock River in June 1772*], Runaway from Rev Mr Boucher in Prince George Co, MD, in Oct last and boasts of having been transported before. From Clement Brooke or Dr Richard Brooke in MD. r(VG 3 Dec 1772).

Cartt, Thomas, no age stated, Runaway Servant who stammers, tailor by trade. From Benjamin Catton of York Town, Va.

Cartwright, John, more than 40, well-made with an impediment in speech, Deserted as gunner of the galley *Norfolk's Revenge* lying in Chickahominy River. From John Calvert of the said vessel. (VG 14 Jun 1776).

Cartwright, Thomas, about 22, [*possibly transported by Gloucestershire Assizes of Lent 1774 for stealing hay*], Runaway Indented English Servant of ruddy complexion, by trade a bricklayer; he is a smooth-spoken modest-looking man who may head for Gwyn's Island as a freeman. From William Shedden, Essex Co, VA. (VG 29 Jun 1776).

Carver, William, 26, Runaway Scottish Indented Servant, stout with white eyebrows and lashes, a sharp nose, long-faced and much pitted with smallpox. From Daniel Grant, Baltimore Town, MD. (VG 7 Apr 1774).

Carwick, John, 18, Runaway Apprentice Boy, slim with a scar on the tip of his nose. From Nicholas B Seabrook, Norfolk, VA. (VG 5 Jan 1775).

Ceaton, John, no age given, [*transported from Middlesex Quarter Sessions in 1767 by the* Tryal], Runaway English Convict Servant, has crooked toes and a red coloured wig. From Adam Reaburn near Stanton, Augusta, VA. (VG 18 Oct 1770).

Celsey, Steycker, about 40, Runaway Indented Servant who says he was born in England and pretends to be a ship carpenter and caulker, has snagged teeth, is apt to stutter, fond of drink, appears quiet but is as great a rogue as ever trod the earth. From Micajah James in Baltimore Town, MD. (VG 25 Oct 1776).

Chambers, John, about 21, [*probably transported either from Warwickshire Assizes in 1767 or Hampshire Assizes in 1765*], Runaway English Convict Servant with bandy legs. From Henry James and Mordecai Gist in Baltimore, MD.(VG 5 Apr 1770).

Chamblis, John, 38, thin-faced with commonly sore eyes caused by hard drinking. Runaway Deserter from 6th Battalion of Continental Regulars. From Capt James Johnson of said Battalion, Swan's Point, VA. (VG 26 Jul 1776).

Chance, William, no age given, Deserter from Capt John Blair's Co of 9th Virginia Regiment when under marching orders. From Lieut Thomas Overton, Williamsburg, VA. (VG 11 Jul 1777).

Chandler, Charles Winfrie, 17, Runaway Servant. From James Gardener, carpenter of Williamsburg, VA. (VG 18 Mar & 19 Aug 1773).

Chapman, Cornelius, 19, Deserter from Camp at Maidstone, VA, born in MD. From Commanding Officer, Winchester, VA. (VG 27 Aug 1756).

Charles, Lewis Jr, no age given, Suspected Runaway Soldier Deserter who served for 6 months in the Army before returning home and re-enlisting on assurance he would serve as sergeant major in the Commonwealth Service. From W Stark, Brunswick Co, VA. (VG 8 Aug 1777).

Charlick (Charlock), Nicholas, no age stated, [*transported from Cornwall to Queen Anne's Co, MD, by Amity in 1737*], a West Country man, mason by trade. From Patrick Creagh, Annapolis, MD. (VG 30 Jun – 7 Jul 1738).

Cheathum, Josiah, about 22, Runaway Deserter from 6th Virginia Regiment at College Camp. From Capt Samuel Cabell. (VG 5 Jul 1776).

Chelson, Stephen, about 19, a Virginian having served apprenticeship as carpenter & joiner. From James Rob of Lancaster Co, VA. (VG 24-31 Jul 1746).

Childers, John, no age given, of Halifax Co, VA, Runaway Deserter Recruit raised for the Georgia Service. From Robert & George Walton at Prince Edward Courthouse. (VG 27 Sep 1776).

Childs, William, about 21, [*sentenced to be transported by Middlesex Sessions in Jan-Feb 1774*], Runaway English Servant, a carver and gilder. From William Smithson near Bush River, Harford Co, MD. (VG 21 Apr 1775).

Clark, David, no age stated, Irish Servant, woolcomber and tobacco spinner who ran away from claimant Alexander Ramsay of Marsh Creek, York Co, PA, and was committed to Alexandria Prison, Fairfax Co, VA, but broke out. (VG 1 Aug 1771).

Clark, James, about 28, Runaway Irish Convict Servant who talks broken English. From James Mountgomery of Rockfish Settlement Amherst Co, VA. (VG 22 Dec 1768).

Clark, John, no age given, Runaway English Servant who pretends to be a ship carpenter or sawyer or founder; he may make for Edenton, NC, pretending he has a brother resident there as a carver. From John Mercer of Marlborough, Stafford Co, VA. (VG 2 May 1755).

Clark, Samuel, about 33, Indentured English Servant imported from London in the *Lord Camden*, Capt John Johnston; he has a wide mouth and long teeth and is pretty talkative, by trade a cooper. From George Leslie of Portsmouth, VA. (VG 26 Jan 1769).

Clarke, Stephen, about 33, Runaway Indented Servant stooped in his walk, a tailor by trade supposed to have gone to NC or to Sir Payton Shipwith's plantation on the Roanoake where his wife's brother Robert Reader lives and who came into the country on the same ship two years ago. From Joshua Storrs of Richmond, VA. (VG 5 Dec 1771 & 6 Feb 1772).

Clarke, Walter, about 21, Suspected Runaway Irish Servant detained in Williamsburg public jail, supposedly a servant of John Campbell, merchant near New London, Bedford Co; he is a pert forward fellow. The owner to contact the jailer Peter Pelham. (VG 9 Feb 1776).

Clay, Percival (Perciball), no age given, [*sentenced at Hull Assizes in Summer 1745 for stealing at Kirk Ella, Yorkshire*], Convict Servant, blacksmith. From Francis Brown, Wicomoco River, Northumberland Co, VA. (VG 24-31 Jul 1746).

Clealing, Andrew, about 25, Suspected Runaway Irish Servant confined to Elizabeth City Jail who has lost an eye and is much marked with smallpox; he carries a pass signed by Charles McCarty thought to be false. Owner to contact the jailer John McLachlin. (VG 20 Oct 1775).

Clean (Clear), Richard, 30-40, Runaway Indented Servant who says he is English but is believed to be Irish with reddish hair, by trade a joiner and house carpenter. From John Augustine Washington or John Turberville, Westmoreland Co, VA.

Clerk, Alexander, no age given, Runaway Scottish Servant who cannot read. From Francis Willis of Gloucester Co, VA. (VG 10 Apr 1752).

Clerk, Patrick, no age stated, Runaway Irish Servant much pitted with smallpox. From Lawrence Washington Sr at Choptank, Stafford Co, VA. (VG 18 Jul 1771).

Clerk, Philip, no age stated, [*probably transported from Middlesex Sessions of Jul 1768 & shipped for 14 years on the Justitia to VA*]. Runaway Irish Convict Servant little marked with smallpox. From Richard Woods of Albemarle Co, VA. (VG 26 Jan 1769).

Clerk, William, no age given, Runaway surgeon from the snow *Fortune*, Capt. William Rowntree, lately wrecked in Chesapeake Bay. From George Brown, of Kingston, VA. (VG 5 Oct 1769).

Clubb, Alexander, no age given [*transported for life from Kent Assizes by the* Thornton *in Apr 1772*], Runaway English Convict Servant, well-made, six feet tall, has been some time in the Army and is a shoemaker. From John Kidd, Commander of the *Thornton* lying at Leeds Town, VA. (VG 23 Jul 17

Coboggen, Peter Goffegon, about 22. From Maximilian Grimes, Portsmouth, VA. (VG 30 Jan 1772).

Cockle (Cockil), John, about 25, [*transported from London Sessions by the* Justitia *in 1767*] a little pitted with smallpox, Runaway Servant who has followed the water since he was a boy and has stolen a boat, supposedly to go to Beaufort, NC, but by trade a hairdresser. He has been 4-5 years in the country, and is very talkative and ready of speech. From John Atkinson of Fredericksburg, VA. (VG 19 Mar 1772).

Cole, James, no age given, Runaway Convict Servant, bricklayer by trade, very talkative with an insolent and daring aspect when provoked; he has lost the forefinger of his right hand. From Richard Lee of the Naval Office, Charles Co, MD.(VG 24 Oct 1751).

Cole, Richard (1751) – *See* Horn.

Cole, William, about 24, Servant. From Richard Snowden, Patuxent Iron Works, MD. (VG 15-22 Jun 1739).

Cole, William (1739) – *See* Burnett.

Coleman alias Nabb, John, no age given, transported from Surrey Assizes in 1737 by the *Forward*. Runaway Convict and frequent offender in England, bow-legged, sly, pretended shoemaker by trade. From John Ralls, Caroline Co, VA. (VG 22-29 Sep 1738).

Colley, William, no age given, Suspected Deserter from Deep Spring Camp, VA, of 6th Virginia Regiment. Warning from Capt James Johnson of said Regt. (VG 30 Aug 1776).

Collins, John alias Butler, John, no age given, Runaway Irish Servant with a large scar on the end of his nose. From Matthew Mayes Jr of Price George Co, VA. (VG 30 Nov-7 Dec 1739); from Charles Carter of Richland Farm of King George Co, VA. (VG 7-14 Dec 1739).

Colloney, Richard, alias O'Daniel, James, no age given. Runaway Irish Servant. From Robert Rennolds near Port Royal, Caroline Co, VA. (VG 29 Sep 1774).

Colton, William, no age stated. Runaway Indented Servant, slim made with inflamed eyes probably caused by smallpox. From John Augustine Washington or John Turberville, Westmoreland Co, VA. (VG 26 Jul 1775).

Commodore, John (1770) – *See* Holmes

Connel alias Sullivane, Margaret, 40-50, Irish Convict Servant speaks the brogue. From Richard Taylor of Petersburg, VA. (VG 19 Sep 1755).

Conneran, Thomas, 20, Runaway Irish Soldier Deserter from 2nd Virginia Regiment in NJ. From Col Alexander Spotswood of said Regiment. (VG 5 Sep 1777).

Connor, John, no age stated, Runaway Irish Servant, talks in brogue, poxridden and redheaded sailmaker, came from Bristol in ship *Essex*, Capt Henry Morgan. From Patrick Creagh of Annapolis, MD. (VG 8-15 Oct 1736).

Connor, John, no age stated, Runaway Irish Servant, talks in brogue, poxridden and redheaded sailmaker, came from Bristol in ship *Essex*, Capt Henry Morgan. From Patrick Creagh of Annapolis, MD. (VG 8-15 Oct 1736).

Conner, Thomas, no age given, Runaway Irish Convict Servant who retains much of the brogue. From Richard Woods of Albemarle Co, VA. (VG 26 Jan 1769).

Conner, Peter, no age given, Runaway Irish Indented Servant who walks like a sailor and has lately been whipped for threatening a man's life, the scars from which still show near his navel. From James Briden, Goochland Courthouse, VA. (VG 14 Jun 1776).

Conoly, William, 16-17, Runaway Irish Convict Servant, pert looking with a scar on his face from the kick of a horse. From Robert Adam of Alexandria, VA. (VG 23 Jul 1767).

Conroy, Michael, about 25, Runaway Irish Convict Servant, much freckled and pitted with smallpox, pretends to be a shoemaker. From Isaac Short near Snoden's Ironworks, Prince George Co, MD. (VG 21 Sep 1775).

Cooley, John, about 22, Runaway English Servant, round faced and well set. From Thomas Bond living near Bush River, Harford Co, MD. (VG 21 Apr 1775).

Constantine, Edward?, 19, Deserter from Camp at Maidstone, VA, born in MD. From Commanding Officer, Winchester, VA. (VG 27 Aug 1756).

Cooper, William, no age given, of Pittsylvania, VA, Runaway Deserter Recruit raised for the Georgia Service. From Robert & George Walton at Prince Edward Courthouse. (VG 27 Sep 1776).

Copper, Thomas, no age given, Suspected Runaway English Lad committed to Amherst Gaol , VA. Owner to apply to gaoler William Pollard. (VG 21 Sep 1776).

Corgan, James, 26-27, Runaway Irish Servant with reddish beard, much pox-pitted and having little of the brogue, a pretty good sailor. From Anthony Haden, Albemarle Co, VA. (VG 21 Mar 1771).

Cornee, Conner, about 30, Suspected Runaway Irish Servant who says he was landed in SC from a ship commanded by Capt Wilson for which he had paid his passage. Owner to contact William Bell, gaoler of Orange Co Gaol, VA. (VG 13 May 1773).

Cosgrave, John, no age given, Runaway Servant, much pitted with smallpox who ran from the ship *Becky* in James River, VA, and has been seen in Roanoake. From James Buchanan of said ship. (VG 12 Mar 1752).

Cooke, Henry, about 24, Runaway Free Negro Servant who was born in Gloucester Co, VA, but indented himself for 5 years to cure a pox. From William Flood, Westmoreland, VA. (VG 19 Apr 1770).

Cooper, Edmund, about 40, [weaver of Middleton, Lancashire, who was tried for returning from transportation but, for lack of evidence was ordered away again and taken to VA by the *Justitia* in1768], Convict Servant well instructed in learning and law who wore a steel collar when he went, last seen in Urbanna (in 1769). From James Laird of Augusta, VA. (VG 14 Apr 1768 & 7 Sep 1769).

Cooper, Thomas, about 25, claims to be Yorkshire born and "talks broad." From James Maginess, Orange Co, VA. (VG 24 Mar 1768).

Coulter, James, about 25, Suspected Runaway Servant in Staunton Gaol, VA. Apply to Gaoler Thomas Rhodes. (VG 10 Mar 1774).

Coupland, Joseph, about 20, Runaway recruit from King William Co who has a stooped walk, shoemaker by trade and is supposed gone to Prince Edward Co, VA. From John Russel of King William Co. (VG 28 Feb 1755).

Cowan, Elizabeth, about 50, Runaway Scottish Convict Servant. From Caleb Worley and Hugh Allen, Botetourt, VA. (VG 2 Dec 1773).

Cowen, Israel, about 27, [*transported for 14 years from London Sessions in 1767 for receiving stolen goods, transported to VA in Sep 1767 by the* Justitia], Runaway English Convict Servant, bald headed and blind in left eye. From Robert Whitley and John Maxwell in forks of James River, Augusta Co, VA. (VG 16 Jun 1768).

Cowgill, John, about 25, Runaway Indented Servant, thick well set and used to the sea. From John Harris in Hanover, VA. (VG 22 Jul 1773).

Cox, William, about 17, Runaway English Servant Boy who stoops much and has a most villainous countenance; lately seen in King and Queen Co, VA. From Andrew Crawford, Hobb's Hole, VA. (VG 16 May 1771).

Coxall, William Cavalier, about 20, Indented English Servant imported by the *Lord Camden* last fall from London, says he was born in West Indies, brought up in London & belongs to George Tuberville of Westmoreland Co, VA. From Daniel Morgan of Westmoreland Co, VA. (VG 8 Nov 1770).

Craggs, Anthony, no age given, Suspected Runaway Servant from Annapolis, MD, a barber and farrier, a young man supposed to belong to Joseph Galloway. The owner to apply to John Lyne, gaoler of Frederick Co Gaol. (VG 2 Aug 1770).

Craig, George, between 30 and 40, Scottish gardener and indented servant. From John Augustine Washington or John Turberville, Westmoreland Co, VA. (VG 26 Jul 1775).

Craig, Robert, no age given, [*possibly the one of that name sentenced to transportation by Middlesex Quarter Sessions in Feb 1761*], Runaway Scottish Servant weaver with a very broad dialect. From William Briggs near Dumfries, Prince William Co, VA. (VG 10 Dec 1767).

Craighead, Robert, no age stated, Deserter from Camp at Maidstone, VA, born in MD. From Commanding Officer, Winchester, VA. (VG 27 Aug 1756).

Crap, Richard, no age given, Runaway tailor from the snow *Fortune*, Capt. William Rowntree, lately wrecked in Chesapeake Bay. From George Brown, of Kingston, VA. (VG 5 Oct 1769).

Crawley (Cralle), Rodham Kenner, 18, Runaway English Apprentice Lad, slender made and a little round-shouldered who has served about 4 years as a house joiner but knows little about it. From William Gresham in Northumberland, VA. (VG 2 Dec 1773); aged 21, 6 feet 1 inch tall, slender and round-shouldered, Runaway Deserter Soldier, of 5th Battalion, Williamsburg, who took part in a mutiny. From Capt Thomas Gaskins Jr, Williamsburg. (VG 27 Sep 1776).

Crew, Josiah, about 24, who has red eyes. Runaway Deserter from 6th Regiment of Continental Regulars. From Nicholas Hobson of said Regiment. (VG 26 Jul 1776).

Croson, James, no age given, Runaway English Servant of small stature and pitted with smallpox. From Robert Stobo of Petersburg, VA. (VG 21 Aug 1752).

Croson, Robert, about 26, Runaway Servant born in VA, was formerly taken up in Charles City Co but was whipped and discharged. From William Wyatt, Williamsburg, VA. (VG 8-11 Oct 1736 & 1-8 Apr 1737).

Crouch, Richard, about 25, [*transported for life from Wiltshire Assizes in 1769*], Runaway Convict Servant, much pitted with smallpox, low in speech, who has supposedly gone towards NC as he is convicted for life. From Anne Middleton of Annapolis, MD. (VG 9 May 1771).

Crump, Jesse, about 19, Runaway English Apprentice Lad, a tailor by trade with a stooped walk. From Bennett White, Newcastle, VA. (VG 9 & 23 Sep 1773).

Crump, Lyddal, 17, Runaway Apprentice Boy from the plantation of John Parke Custis in King & Queen Co., VA. From George Clopton Jr. (VG 4 Aug 1775).

Cuddy, William, about 38, Runaway marked with smallpox & with a blind right eye, last heard of in Brunswick Co, NC, and may return there. From John Shortwell of Orange Co, VA. (VG 19-26 Sep 1745).

Cullen, John, no age given, Runaway Irish Servant, a young man recently arrived in the country and belonging to Charles Hammond Jr. (VG 26 Jul 1770).

Cullen, Mary (1738) - *See* Tool, Darby.

Curtis, James, no age given, [*sentenced to 14 years' transportation by Middlesex Sessions in Oct 1768 & shipped to VA in Feb 1769 by the* Thornton], Apprentice Boy supposedly gone towards Dumplin Island, Nansemond Co, VA. From William Row of a little above West Poit, King William Co, VA. (VG 1 Aug 1771).

Cuthbert, Alexander, about 22, Runaway Scottish Servant born in Perth who was for some time in England and has little accent, by trade a bricklayer who came in to Potomac River on Capt Grigg's ship; he has probably gone northwards. From William Black of Price George Co, VA. (VG 3 Dec 1767).

Dames, Charles, no age given, Runaway Seaman who acted as Steward on the ship *Brilliant*, supposedly gone to his uncle John Dames at Old Point Comfort. From James Miller of said ship at Cumberland, VA. (VG 7 Jul 1774).

Dancer, John, about 25, Runaway Mulatto Servant who writes well and may use that qualification to pass for a freeman. From John Hipkins, King & Queen Co, VA. (VG 18 Feb 1775).

Daniel, Andrew, about 20, Runaway Soldier Deserter from the French Co in Williamsburg, VA, who has a long thin face, short reddish hair and speaks a little broken English. From La Giroruete, Williamsburg, VA. (VG 22 Aug 1777).

Daniel, Edward alias McDonald, James, about 50, Runaway Irish Convict Servant just imported by the *Justitia* for highway robbery; was convicted some years ago but escaped. From Benjamin Grymes Jr near Fredericksburg, Spotsylvania Co, VA. (VG 16 Feb 1769).

D'Anvers, John, about 30, pitted with smallpox and frequently seized with trembling fits, pretends to be a barber by trade. From Robert Lyon of Williamsburg, VA. (VG 4 Apr 1755).

Darcy, Thomas, about 28, Suspected Runaway Servant, a tanner and currier by trade, full faced and well-set who says he is a freeman, now committed to Augusta Gaol. Owner, if any, to apply to gaoler Thomas Rhoades. (VG 10 Feb 1774).

Davis, Charles, 18-20, Runaway English Convict Servant, short and squat with a large scar on his head who is well known on Rappahannock as a waiting man. From James Laverty, Fredericksburg, VA. (VG 22 Sep 1768).

Davis, David, about 20, Runaway Apprentice Lad who walks very straight and is much marked with smallpox, by trade a cabinet maker. From Benjamin Bucktrout in Williamsburg, VA. (VG 4 Apr 1771).

Davis, Henry, no age stated, Runaway Seaman from the *Virginian*, Capt Richard Lewis, at Littlepage's Landing, New Kent Co, VA. (VG 11-18 Apr 1745).

Davis, John, no age given, West Country Servant lately imported from Bristol, tall and thin, looks like a labouring person, probably gone North having formerly lived in Philadelphia. From Edward Barradall of Williamsburg, VA. (VG 4-11 May 1739).

Davies, John, no age given, Runaway wheelwright from the snow *Fortune*, Capt. William Rowntree, lately wrecked in Chesapeake Bay. From George Brown, of Kingston, VA. (VG 5 Oct 1769).

Davis alias Philips, Mary, middle-aged, Runaway Convict Servant, stout, swarthy and much pitted with smallpox, always talks as though she has a bad cold and poses as a beggar who has lost her husband and has two children to maintain; she will probably make for Rappahannock. From John Catlett, near Todd's Bridge, King William Co, VA. (VG 21 Jan & 4 Mar 1773).

Davis, Nathan, 17, Runaway Country-born Apprentice, clumsy made with a downcast look, bloated face, hollow eyes and fond of liquor; he is now a soldier in Capt Nelson's company at York, VA. From John McDowgal at the lower end of Hanover, VA. (VG 9 Aug 1776).

Davis, Philip, about 24, Runaway Servant from Lancashire who speaks the dialect. From James Powell, New Town, Eastern Branch of Elizabeth River, VA. (VG 6-13 Oct 1738).

Davis, Richard, no age given, [*probably transported from Surrey Assizes by* Justitia *in 1765.*] Runaway English Convict Servant who speaks thick, watch and clock mender, believed to have gone to Rappahannock. From Edward Hill of Prince George Co, VA. (VG 4 & 25 Jul 1766).

Davis, Richard, about 21, Suspected Runaway Servant who says he came from Philadelphia. Owner to apply to John Purcell, gaoler of Richmond Co Gaol, VA. (VG 27 Sep 1770).

Davis, Thomas, about 24, born in Wales, Runaway Servant, bricklayer. From Theophilus Pugh of Nansemond Co, VA, merchant. (VG 10-17 Jun 1737).

Davis, Thomas, no age given, slender and much pitted with smallpox, Runaway Deserter Seaman of sloop of war *Scorpion*. From Wright Westcott, Yeocomico, VA. (VG 23 Aug 1776).

Davis, William, no age listed, native of Great Britain, Deserted from Pittsylvania Regular Company in Williamsburg. From Capt Thomas Hutchings, Headquarters, Williamsburg, VA. (VG 24 May 1776).

Davis, Thomas, about 40, Convict Welsh Black Servant. From ship *Duke of Cumberland* at Bermuda Hundred, James River, VA. From Joseph Barnes, master of said ship. (VG 18-25 May 1739).

Dawson, George, no age stated, Runaway Seaman from the *Virginian*, Cdr Richard Lewis, at Littlepage's Landing, New Kent Co, VA. (VG 11-18 Apr 1745).

Dawson, John, 24, Deserter from Camp at Maidstone, VA, born in MD. From Commanding Officer, Winchester, VA. (VG 27 Aug 1756).

Day, William, no age given, Runaway English Convict Servant [*transported from Middlesex Sessions by* Scarsdale *in Jul 1771*), middle-aged and middle-sized, very swarthy, fast talking, who was brought up to the farming business. From Gerard B Causin, four miles below Port Tobacco, MD. (VG 6 Feb 1772).

Daylies, William & Hannah, Runaway Irish Convict Servants who ran after working in Richmond Co, Va; both are tinkers who said they lived in Augusta, VA. From William Taite of Northumberland Co, VA. (VG 26 Mar 1767).

Dayly, Charles, about 21, Runaway Irish Convict Servant who walks nimbly and talks fierce. From Thomas Blincoe and Hardage Lane of Loudoun Co, VA. (VG 18 Jan 1770).

Dean, Hugh, about 21, Runaway Irish Convict Servant, much pitted with smallpox, with a roguish look, pretends to be a German, plays well on the violin and is a great drunkard; he says he was brought up as a metal refiner, chemist and doctor; last seen on Rappahannock River near Port Royal, VA. From Morgan Graven of Hanover Co, VA. (VG 4 Jul 1751).

Deane, Jones Allen, about 13, Apprentice Lad with remarkably large eyes who speaks quick and is very saucy. From John Saunders of Williamsburg, VA. (VG 21 Jun 1770).

Dean, Joshua, about 40, [sentenced to death but reprieved at London Sessions to be transported for life for forging stamps & shipped to VA in Sep 1736 by the *Dorsetshire*], runaway from Germanna, VA, in Jun 1737. From Alexander Spotswood, Postmaster General of America. (VG 4-11 Aug 1738).

Dean, Julias, no age given. Deserter from Capt Nathaniel Cocke's Co of 7th Virginia Regiment. From Lieut Tarpley White, Williamsburg, VA. (VG 28 Mar 1777).

Dean, William, no age given. Deserter from Capt Nathaniel Cocke's Co of 7th Virginia Regiment. From Lieut Tarpley White, Williamsburg, VA. (VG 28 Mar 1777).

Defoos, Micajah, no age given, Runaway Soldier Deserter from 2nd Georgia Battalion who enlisted in Williamsburg, VA. From Lieut Robert Ward, Williamsburg. (VG 24 Jan 1777).

Delk, Benjamin, no age given, Runaway Soldier Deserter from 2nd Georgia Battalion who enlisted in Williamsburg, VA. From Lieut Robert Ward, Williamsburg. (VG 24 Jan 1777).

Delks, Dudley, about 24, Runaway Mulatto Soldier born in NC, enlisted at Brunswick. From William Gooch at Williamsburg Camp.(VG 24-31 Jul 1746).

Denny, William, about 30, round-shouldered, much pitted with smallpox and fond of liquor, Runaway Irish Soldier Deserter from 2nd Virginia Regiment in NJ. From Col Alexander Spotswood of said Regiment. (VG 5 Sep 1777).

Devereaux (Deverix), James, 20, [*transported for 14 years from Middlesex Sessions by the* Justitia *in Jan 1774 for violent theft*]. English Runaway Servant who has a crooked nose occasioned by a blow; his design is probably "to enlist under pretence of being a Friend to the Glorious Cause of America, but means only to desert when opportunity serves." From William Wyatt on Kettle Run, Prince William Co, VA. (VG 29 Jun 1776).

Devoux, Stephen, about 20, [*transported in 1765 by the* Tryal *from Middlesex Sessions*]. Runaway Convict Servant, by trade a baker, grim looking and much pitted with smallpox. From Robert Adam of Alexandria, Fairfax Co, VA. (VG 6 Jun 1766).

Dickerson, William, young fellow, Runaway Soldier Deserter who "was born in Gloucester County where I have some reason to believe he was persuaded by some Tory that he could not be compelled to continue in the service" but ran from a company of regulars stationed at York, VA. From Capt Charles Tomkies, Williamsburg, VA. (VG 25 Oct 1776). Response by the father David Dickerson who says he can prove his son is still under 16 and was enlisted without his consent but the illness of his wife obliged him to seek his release. The writer is a warm friend to his country and not a Tory. (VG 8 Nov 1776).

Diggens, Daniel (1774) – *See* Dunn.

Dinkins, Theophilus, about 40, Runaway Soldier Deserter from 3rd Regiment of NC enlisted in Bute Co, NC, tall. From Lieut William Linton. (VG 9 May 1777).

Dixon, John, 19-20, Runaway Servant who says he was born in England but is supposed to be Irish, by trade a smith who delights in making clasp knives. From John Hobday of Gloucester Co. (VG 10 Oct 1755).

Dobey (Dobby), James, about 40, [*sentenced at London Sessions in Feb for stealing a coat & transported in Apr 1765 to VA on the ship* Ann], Runaway English Convict Servant, shy, artful, talkative with a large grey beard, a sailor pitted with smallpox. From Charles G Griffith & Henry Griffith Jr of Seneca, Frederick Co, MD. (VG 16 Jun 1768).

Dobson, Robert (1763) – *See* Hobday.

Dolan, Bridget, no age given, Irish Servant pitted with smallpox. From Joseph Gilliam of Williamsburg, VA. (VG 24-31 Jul 1746).

Dolton, Christopher, about 25, Runaway Irish Convict Servant, clumsy made, stoop-shouldered and pitted with smallpox. From Andrew Hamilton, Calf Pasture, Augusta, VA. (VG 15 Aug 1771).

Donahow, Patrick, no age given, Runaway Irish Servant, a little bald with a black beard. From Jacob Andrew Minitree of Charles Co, Potomac, MD. (VG 7 Mar 1751).

Donaldson, Ebenezer, no aged given, Runaway Scottish Indented Servant who ran from the *Greenvale* at Ruffin's Ferry, Pamunky River. From Thomas Ritchie of the said ship. (VG 19 Apr 1770).

Donaldson, William, no age given, [possibly the one of that name sentenced at London Sessions in Apr1775 to be transported for stealing a shirt and shipped to MD in Jul 1775 by the Saltpring], Suspected Runaway Servant who fell sick on his way to gaol and cannot therefore be described. Application to be made to John Lyne, gaoler of Winchester, Frederick Co, VA. (VG 13 Sep 1770).

Donally, Henry, about 17, Runaway Irish Servant. From Mary Bordland, Hampton, VA. (VG 3-10 Dec 1736).

Donoho, James, nearly 30, portly with a down look and the remains of an old sore on one leg, probably gone to Bedford Co where his parents live near New London, VA. Runaway deserter from armed vessel *Muskito*, Capt Isaac Younghusband, lying at Warwick. From Jacob Valentine in Richmond Town, VA. (VG 28 Jun 1776).

Donowho alias Quinn, John, no age given, Runaway Servant who has lived as a waterman in George Town, VA, for 4-5 months with a pass from Mr Buchanan of Baltimore. From Thomas Rigden in George Town, VA. (VG 7 & 21Oct 1773).

Dorton, William, no age given, of Williamsburg, VA. Deserter from Capt Smith's Co of 2nd Georgia Battalion who served in 2nd Virginia Regt under Capt R.K.Meade, then enlisted under Lieut Mason. From Lieut Alexander Baugh of Cumberland Courthouse, VA. (VG 21 Feb 1777).

Doten, John, about 30, Runaway Irish Servant with a brogue who pretends to be a maltster and brewer, now supposedly among the Cherokee Indians. From Daniel Hornby, Williamsburg, VA. (VG 14-21 Oct 1737).

Douglas, James, about 32, Scottish Indented Servant, stout, surly-faced, a little pock marked, speaks a thick Scots dialect, by trade a brass founder; he is said to have gone towards Philadelphia. From Samuel Kempton, Norfolk, VA. (VG 5 Jan 1775).

Downrichards, Thomas, no age given, Runaway Servant. From Thomas Green near the Sugar Lands, Frederick Co, MD. (VG 21 Sep 1769).

Doyle, John, about 30, Runaway Deserter from HMS *Fowey* in Hampton Road, VA. From Policarous Taylor, Capt of said ship. (VG 3-10 Oct 1745).

Doyl, Thomas, no age given. Runaway Maryland Servant who says he is a sailor who ran away from his ship in New York. The owner should apply to John Lyne, Gaoler of Frederick Co, MD. (VG 8 Mar 1770).

Doyle, Thomas, no age given, (*probably transported for stealing bread by the Suffolk Assizes in Lent 1773*) Runaway Irish Servant belonging to John Ballendine who is desired to apply for his release to Peter Pelham of Williamsburg Public Jail, VA. (VG 3 May 1776).

Driscoll, Michael, about 14, smart looking fellow who talks much in the Irish brogue, imported this year in the *Burwell*, Capt Huison, from Dublin but deserted from the *Carlisle* on James River, VA. From John Towers of the *Carlisle*. (VG 3 Sep 1756).

Driver, John, Runaway Servant who calls himself English, speaks thick and with an Irish accent. From John Atkinson & James Newton in Fredericksburg, VA. (VG 9 Dec 1773).

Drought, Joseph, no age stated, Runaway Convict with thick lips, a smith by trade. From Thomas Ingalls of St. Mary's River, MD, joiner. (VG 24-31 Oct 1745).

Drum, Bryon, no age given, Runaway Irish Servant of ruddy complexion with a scar from mouth to ear on his left cheek. From Philip Cassay, Frederick Co, MD. (VG 18 Feb 1775).

Drury, Timothy, 16-17, Runaway Convict Servant Boy (*transported by the* Justitia *from Middlesex Sessions in Dec 1769*), small for his age, arch and smart. From William Triplet two miles above Leeds Town, VA. (VG 26 Sep 1771).

Dryberry (Drybrow), Thomas, no aged stated, Runaway English Convict Servant (*transported from Surrey Assizes by the* Justitia *in December 1770*), a tall stout fellow with a bloated face who belongs to William Allan adjoining the advertiser's plantation. From James Duncanson of Culpeper, VA. (VG 23 Apr 1772).

Dryshill, Francis, 33, Runaway Irish Soldier Deserter from 2nd Virginia Regiment in NJ, he chews tobacco and is very fond of liquor. From Col Alexander Spotswood of said Regiment. (VG 5 Sep 1777).

Duberg, Edward alias Underwood, John, no age given, former sailor who says he was brought up in Cambridge, England, and speaks several languages; he came in the *Success's Increase* to Rappahannock where he was sold as a schoolmaster. From Richard Lee, Westmoreland Co, VA. (VG 12 May 1774).

Ducret, John Victoire, no age given, (*transported from Middlesex Sessions for life by the* Justitia *in Jan 1775)*, native of Berne, Switzerland who speaks French, English and Italian, almost as dark as a mulatto, a barber by trade; he has a swollen testicle occasioned by a kick he got aboard the *Justitia*, From Richard Graham, Dumfries, VA. (VG 21 Jul 1775).

Duff, Arthur, about 30, Convict Servant, much freckled redhead. From William Kelly of Orange Co, VA. (VG 17-24 Apr 1746).

Duff, James, no age given, Runaway English Servant of dull complexion, thick, sturdy and pitted with smallpox. From John Trimble in Augusta Co, VA. (VG 15 Jun 1775).

Duffy, Patrick, no age given, Runaway Irish Soldier Deserter from 2nd Georgia Battalion who was supposed to be in the marine service. From Capt William Smith, Williamsburg, VA. (VG 6 Dec 1776).

Dugal, Elizabeth, about 27, Runaway Servant pitted with smallpox, has a long nose and says she was born in Pa to which or to Carolina she will probably go. From Lemuel Roberts, Broad Creek, Norfolk Co, VA. (VG 27 Sep 1770).

Duncan, Joseph, no age given, of Bute Co, NC, blacksmith, who confessed to stealing a runaway negro slave belonging to John Mayo of Cumberland Co, VA, who he sold to a Richard Sears; order from Jethro Sumner, Justice of Peace for Bute, for detention of said Duncan believed to reside in Fauquier Co, VA. (VG 18 Jan 1770).

Dunn alias Diggens, Daniel, about 38, Runaway Convict Servant, nailer by trade and calls himself a batten or small rail maker; has worked as a blacksmith at Dumfries and Fredericksburg, VA, and proposed to go to Virginia to change his name to Daniel Diggens. From Samuel Willits c/o Postmaster at Bush Town, MD. (RG 10 Nov 1774).

Durrant, James, no age given, Runaway shipwright from the snow *Fortune*, Capt. William Rowntree, lately wrecked in Chesapeake Bay. From George Brown, of Kingston, VA. (VG 5 Oct 1769).

Eage, Edward, no age given, Runaway Servant, six feet tall and swarthy. From William Withers, Fauquier Co, Ca. (VG 23 Apr 1772).

Ealing, Samuel, Runaway Convict (*transported for life from Surrey Assizes by the* Forward *in 1738*), small thin youth, carpenter and joiner by trade, supposedly gone to Accomack. From William Walker of Westmoreland Co, VA. (VG 29 Jun- 6 Jul 1739).

Early, James, a young middle-sized indented barber who ran from the ship *Chance*, Capt Campbell. From Brown, Grierson & Co, Norfolk, VA. (VG 12 Aug 1773).

Easton, Thomas, Indented Scottish Servant imported in Feb 1774 by the *Betsy*, Richmond, Capt Nivel; he talks much in the dialect and his fore teeth are very irregular. From John Randall, Williamsburg, VA. (VG 7 Jul 1774).

Eaton alias Walker, Alice, about 20, Runaway English Convict Servant who passes as the wife of John Eaton (q.v.), well set woman (*transported as Alice Walker from London Sessions by the* Justitia *in Jan 1773*)

Eaton, George, 20, Runaway English Convict Servant born in London and imported in Feb 1768 from Middlesex Sessions by the *Neptune*, by trade a cabinet maker. From William Porter & Thomas Miller of Fredericksburg, VA. (VG 22 Sep 1768).

Eaton, John, about 25, English Convict Servant, ship carpenter, reprieved at Surrey Assizes in 1772 and transported by the *Justitia* to VA in 1773. From Sampson & George Matthews of Richmond, VA. (VG 27 May & 12 Aug 1773).

Eils, Thomas, no age given, Suspected Runaway Servant in Staunton Gaol, VA. Apply to Gaoler Thomas Rhodes. (VG 10 Mar 1774).

Elder, Donald, no age given, Runaway Scottish Highland Convict Servant who ran from the ship *Donald* at Four Mile Creek, Richmond, VA, in his own country garb. From James McDowall and Robert Burton in Richmond. (VG 15 Apr 1773).

Elder, William, no age given, Runaway Scottish Highland Convict Servant who ran from the ship *Donald* at Four Mile Creek, Richmond, VA, in his own country garb. From James McDowall and Robert Burton in Richmond. (VG 15 Apr 1773).

Ellas, Thomas, no age given, Runaway carver from the snow *Fortune*, Capt. William Rowntree, lately wrecked in Chesapeake Bay. From George Brown, of Kingston, VA. (VG 5 Oct 1769).

Elliot, William, no age given, Runaway English Convict Servant, middle sized and marked with smallpox, a farmer from the north of England who speaks bad English. From James Thompson of the snow *Anne*, Capt Edward Dixon, at Port Royal, VA. (VG 9 Jul 1772).

Ellis, Anne, no age given, Runaway Convict Servant imported in December 1773 in the *Success's Increase*, full-faced lusty woman much addicted to swearing. From H Grymes of Forceput. (VG 7 Apr 1774).

Ellis, Elijah, no age given, Runaway Soldier Deserter from 2nd Battalion for Georgia. From Joseph Pannill, Prince Edward Courthouse, VA. (VG 27 Dec 1776).

Emanuel, Ralph, about 25, Runaway English Convict Servant just imported from London in the *Justitia* (*Sentenced by London Sessions in Dec 1774*), six feet tall and well tressed red hair who has been used to the sea. From Andrew Leitch living in Dumfries, VA. (VG 22 Apr, 29 Apr & 4 May 1775).

Emens, Joseph (1751) – *See* Amens.

Evans, Francis (1739). *See* Powell, David.

Evans, John, no age given, Runaway Welshman who deserted the vessel *Molly* on Hampton River, VA, and supposedly gone towards MD. From James Graham of Hampton.(VG 6 Oct 1752).

Evans, Thomas, no age given, Runaway Sailor who has been two years in VA, chews much tobacco; ran from the *William & Anne*, Capt Strahan, on the Potomack. From David Ross, Williamsburg, VA. (VG 24-31 Jul 1746).

Evrie, John (1770) – *See* Avery.

Ewen (Ewin), John, Convict Servant, about 24 (in 1771), joiner who came into the country in about 1768 (*probably transported by the* Neptune *from Middlesex Quarter Sessions in Dec* 1767); he looks remarkably dull and stupid. From William Buckland, of Richmond Co, VA, master carpenter & joiner. (VG 15 Jun 1769 & 10 Jan 1771).

Faro, John, about 15, Runaway Servant Boy, shoemaker by trade brought in by the ship *Duke of Argyle*, Capt Ludlow. From David Armistead, York Town, VA. (VG 3-10 Apr 1746).

Farrall, Thomas, no age given, Suspected Runaway Servant who says he belongs to Col John Syme at York, VA. Owner to apply to Samuel Portlock, Gaoler of Norfolk Co, VA. (VG 24 Mar 1774).

Farrell, John, about 35, Runaway Irish Convict Servant, sickly looking, pitted by smallpox, with coarse features, stoops much and walks badly; has much of the brogue, by trade a cooper. (*Transported from Southwark Sessions by* Justitia *in 1773*). From McCall & Shedden's Mill, Hobb's Hole, VA. (VG 26 Aug 1773).

Farrill, Thomas, no age given, Runaway Irish Indented Servant, stout made, by trade a tanner. From Miles Taylor, Richmond Town, Henrico Co, VA. (VG 28 Apr 1774).

Fawcett (Phoset), Thomas, no age stated, (*?transported from Durham Quarter Sessions in Lent 1768*); has been little time in the country and is a weaver by trade. From Sampson Dorell near Alexandria, Fairfax Co, VA. (VG 17 Nov 1768).

Fay, Thomas, about 18, Runaway Irish Servant who walks badly. From Freer Armston, Norfolk, VA. (VG 11 Jul 1771).

Fazakerley, James, about 25, marked with smallpox, Lancashire man lately arrived who speaks broad, miller. From Robert Yates of St Mary's Co, MD. (VG 28 Jul – 4 Aug 1738).

Fentress, Nehemiah, no age given, of Norfolk Co, VA, Runaway Soldier Deserter from 15th Continental Battalion. From Capt William Grimes, Williamsburg, VA. (VG 28 Mar 1777).

Fermey, Thomas, no age given, Runaway English Servant who speaks broad, by trade a tailor. From Robert Stobo of Petersburg, VA. (VG 21 Aug 1752).

Ferrell, Thomas, no age given, Runaway Irish Servant, a miller by trade. From William Williams of Culpeper, VA. (VG 11 Apr 1771).

Ferrell, William, about 25, Runaway Irish Convict Servant, 6 feet tall with a strong voice and gives impertinent answers, clothier and dyer by trade, thought to have gone towards Mobjack Bay. From Anthony Strother of Fredericksburg, VA. (VG 17 Jul 1752).

Fiddes, Christopher, no age given, Runaway Irish Convict Servant,(*transported for 14 years from York City Sessions in 1758),* very talkative, boldly behaved, near sighted and drinks too much; slightly marked with smallpox. From Francis Hague near the Quaker Meeting House, Loudoun Co, VA. (VG 2 Nov 1769).

Field, John, 25-26, Runaway English Indented Servant, a hostler or gentleman's servant who says he came from Herefordshire. From William Binsley, Capt of the snow *Castle* lying at York Town, VA. (VG 19 May 1774).

Field, John, no age given, lisps and squints a little, Runaway Sailor who deserted from the ship *Elizabeth* lying at Alexandria, VA, Capt Frederick Baker. From Robert Adam & Co, Williamsburg, VA. (VG 24 Feb 1775).

Field, Thomas alias Langham, James, no age given, Irish Runaway Servant, joiner who ran from William Rand of Gloucester Co, VA, with a bay horse and has lately been seen in Nansemond and the borders of Carolina. From John Dupree, Williamsburg, VA. (VG 10-17 Dec 1736 & 18-25 Feb 1737)).

Fillikins, Abraham, Runaway Virginian Soldier at Williamsburg Camp, VA, 22, has an impudent look and a scar over his left eye. From William Gooch at Williamsburg Camp.(VG 24-31 Jul 1746).

Finch, Comfort , no age given, Runaway Servant from Dorothea Benger of Spotsylvania Co, VA. (VG 28 Feb 1755).

Finch, Richard, no age given, Runaway Servant from Dorothea Benger of Spotsylvania Co, VA. (VG 28 Feb 1755).

Fisher, John, Runaway

. From Edward Smith of Richmond Town, VA. (VG 14 Feb 1771). Servant from Yorkshire with large crooked nose, professed horse jockey. Zachariah Hicks of Bull Hill, Appamattox River, Prince George Co, VA. (VG 13-20 Apr 1739).

Fiskin, Peter, no age given, Runaway Scottish Servant, a tailor by trade. From John Orr, Richmond Town, VA. (VG 23 Apr 1772).

Fitzgerald, Cornelius, no age given, Runaway Soldier Deserter from 2nd Battalion for Georgia. From Joseph Pannill, Prince Edward Courthouse, VA. (VG 27 Dec 1776).

Fitzgerald, Florence, about 19, Runaway Irish Servant Man who writes in a tolerably good hand and who went off with two of his countrymen

Fitzjarrel, Morris (1773) – *See* Keeling, Andrew.

Fleming, James, no age given, Runaway Soldier Deserter from 2nd Battalion for Georgia. From Joseph Pannill, Prince Edward Courthouse, VA. (VG 27 Dec 1776).

Fleming, John, about 27, Runaway Indented English Servant, thin-faced with a sallow complexion, by trade a painter, drawer and silversmith. From Gavin Hamilton, Williamsburg, VA. (VG 17 Jun 1775).

Fleming, Thomas, no age given, Runaway English Servant but talks broken, walks like a sailor and has a very down look. (*Probably transported from Norfolk Assizes in* 1764). From John Callaway, Pittsylvania Co, VA. (VG 12 May 1768).

Fletcher. John, no age given, Runaway Indented English Servant with a large sore on his left leg which smells badly, by trade a tanner. From William Houston of Fredericksburg, VA. (VG 18 Oct & 1 Nov 1770).

Flinn, Thomas, over 18, Suspected Runaway Servant who says he belongs to Thomas Badget near Rocky Ridge, VA. The owner to apply to Samuel Farr of Bedord Jail, VA. (VG 4 Aug 1774).

Flin, Timothy & Anne, no ages stated, husband and wife both born in Ireland: he is short and speaks native brogue; she is young and lusty with red hair. From Walter Stewart of Looney's Ferry in Augusta Co, VA. (VG 23 Jun 1768).

Flood, Patrick, no age stated, Runaway Irish Servant, tall and lusty, baker by trade who speaks good English. From John Mitchell of Urbanna, Middlesex Co, VA. (VG 10-17 Mar 1738).

Flower, Matthew, 20, Deserter from Camp at Maidstone, VA, born in MD. From Commanding Officer, Winchester, VA. (VG 27 Aug 1756).

Fogg, William, about 23, Runaway Indented Servant who served his time in London under a blacksmith, six feet tall. From Edward Travis on Poplar Creek, Brunswick Co, VA. (VG 25 Aug 1774).

Foley, Darby, no age stated, Irish Convict Servant. From John Fitzgerald of King William Co, VA. (VG 30 May– 6 Jun 1745).

Forbes, John, about 50, Suspected Runaway Servant who says he belongs to John Hook in NC, thick made of reddish complexion. Owner to apply to Samuel Farr at Bedford Jail. (VG 28 Jul 1774).

Forbes, William, about 20, Runaway Apprentice Boy with stooped shoulders who treads a little knock-kneed and, when drunk, imitates an Irish accent. From John Murphree in Norfolk, VA. (VG 16 Jun 1774).

Ford, Robert, no age given, of country unknown, Runaway who deserted the vessel *Molly* on Hampton River, VA, and supposedly gone towards MD. From James Graham of Hampton. (VG 6 Oct 1752).

Fort, Jacob, 21, 6 feet 2 inches tall, of Edgecombe Co, NC, Runaway Soldier Deserter from 3rd Regiment of NC Continental Troops. From Capt James Bradby. (VG 9 May 1777).

Foster, James, no age given, Runaway weaver from the snow *Fortune*, Capt. William Rowntree, lately wrecked in Chesapeake Bay. From George Brown, of Kingston, VA. (VG 5 Oct 1769).

Foxwell, Richard, Runaway Deserter Soldier, ruddy complexion, snuffles in his speech, is very talkative and says he is a native of the North; since he ran he has again enlisted and deserted. From Lieut Charles Collier, Williamsburg, VA. (VG 23 May 1777).

Francis, Thomas, no age given, [*Sentenced at Somerset Assizes in Mar 1737 & landed in Kent Co, MD, in Nov 1737 from the ship* Raven], Servant of Edward Holmes of Prince George Co, MD, in gaol at Williamsburg, VA, as runaway. (VG 30 Jun – 7 Jul 1738).

Franklin, John, no age given, has a very ugly down look, Runaway Deserter Soldier from 5th Battalion, enlisted in Williamsburg, but came from Hanover, VA. From Gross Scruggs, Williamsburg. (VG 27 Sep 1776).

Franks, Andrew, about 26, Runaway Convict Servant with a noticeable scar on his breast and pretty fond of strong drink, a ropemaker by trade who can play the violin very well. From William Fearson in Williamsburg, VA. (VG 15 Aug 1771).

Frazer, John, no age given, Runaway Servant believed guilty of robbing Josias Cook of Pittsylvania Co, VA. Instruction by John Wilson for him and two others to be apprehended. (VG 28 Apr 1775).

Frazer, William, about 19, a slender man who lived in Hampton but was born in Chesterfield, VA. Runaway Deserted Soldier who enlisted in Williamsburg for the defence of Georgia but failed to join his company at Newgate, Loudoun Co. From Capt William Lane, Williamsburg. (VG 6 Dec 1776).

Freelove, John, no age stated, redhead gardener and a very great rogue. From John Bushrode of Westmoreland Co, VA. (1-17 Aug 1739).

Freeman, Charles, about 25, Runaway English Deserter from the galley *Hero*. From Capt George Muter of said vessel. (VG 26 Jul 1776).

Freeman, William, about 23, stooped shoulders, Runaway Deserted Soldier from Pittsylvania Regular Company in Williamsburg. From Capt Thomas Hutchings, Headquarters, Williamsburg, VA. (VG 24 May 1776).

Freeman, William, no age given, Runaway Soldier Deserter of 6th Virginia Battalion. From the sloop *Susanna* at Leeds Town, VA. From Ensign Harden Perkins, Williamsburg, VA. (VG 18 Oct 1776).

Frye, William, no age stated, Servant who ran away with complainant's wife Mary Sournas, aged about 30, who wears spectacles: they are now supposed to pass as man and wife. From Nicholas Sournas of Stafford Co, VA. (VG 31 Oct 1751).

Fryatt (Fryet), Bartholomew, about 22, [*transported from Ipswich Quarter Sessions, Suffolk, in Jun 1740*)], Runaway Convict Servant, tall and thin with a mole on his right cheek who is fond of his singing. From Charles Carter of Richland Farm, King George Co, VA. (VG 7-14 Dec 1739).

Fullam, Baker, 27, Runaway Servant with 31 years to serve who has a scar on his cheek received from his many villainies, plausible, talkative and impertinent if not checked but a good groom; he may offer his services to Lord Dunmore who "does not object to the colour or condition of any." From Thomas Blackburn near Dumfries, Prince William Co, VA. (VG 1 Dec 1775).

Fullerton, Alexander, about 20, Runaway Scottish Servant who was employed in keeping school, speaks very broad. From Andrew Johnson near Augusta Co Courthouse, VA. (VG 18 Jul 1751).

Furbush, William, no age given, Runaway Apprentice well stocked with assurance. From Bennett White, Williamsburg, VA. (VG 10 Nov 1774).

Gaffney, Terrance and Jane, both about 30, Irish Servants, man and wife purchased from James Porter in MD. The husband understands waiting and hairdressing, his wife has a thin visage. From James Edmondson of Essex Co, VA. (VG 16 Aug & 27 Sep 1770).

Gahagan, John, 43, [*transported for life to VA from Middlesex Sessions in Jul 1773 & shipped to VA in July 1773 in the* Tayloe], Runaway Irish Convict Servant, by trade a grocer, who ran from the said ship at Four Mile Creek, VA. From Sampson & George Mathews, Williamsburg, VA. (VG 11 Nov 1773).

Gales, Charles, about 22, Apprentice Runaway Servant well short and well set. From James Lane near Newgate, Loudoun Co, VA. (VG 2 Dec 1773).

Gardner, Matthew, 50-60, Convict Servant of Bristol much pox-ridden. From ship *Duke of Cumberland* at Bermuda Hundred, James River, VA. From Joseph Barnes, Capt of said ship. (VG 18-25 May 1739).

Gardner, Matthew Jr, about 23, Convict Servant of middle stature who ran from ship *Duke of Cumberland* at Bermuda. From Joseph Barnes, Capt of said ship. (VG 18-15 May 1739).

Gardener, William, born in Caroline Co, VA. Deserter from Capt Thomas Waggoner's Co at Fredericksburg, VA. From Henry Woodward at Fredericksburg. (VG 28 Feb 1755).

Gasford, Samuel (1772) – *See* Carter.

Gelding, Isaac, no age given, Runaway Indentured Servant, short with several moles on his face, a house carpenter by trade, suspected to have gone to Suffolk, VA. From James Southall in Williamsburg, VA. (VG 2 & 4 Mar 1775).

George, William, about 34, Runaway English Servant, [probably the convict of that name sentenced at the Surrey Assizes of Lent 1774 to be transported who was shipped on the *Thornton* to MD in July1774], pockmarked and round-shouldered with a broken left wrist, a carpenter and joiner by trade. (VG 8 Dec 1774).

Gibson alias Johnson, James, no age given, Servant house carpenter & sawyer, cunning noted liar. From Shapleigh Neale, Little Wicomico River, Northumberland Co, VA. (VG 24-31 Oct 1745).

Giddins, Charles, no age given, Runaway Indented Servant, by trade a sawyer who was sent to Williamsburg on business. From Samuel Long in Warwick Co, VA. (VG 2 Jun 1775).

Gilbert, Thomas, 17, apprentice lad. From John Brown, wheelwright near the Capitol, Williamsburg, VA. (VG 14-21 Mar 1745).

Gilding, Isaac, no age given, Runaway English Servant, short, well-made, last seen at Hampton, VA, a house carpenter by trade. From James Southall, Williamsburg, VA. (VG 9 Mar 1775).

Giles, Mary, no age given, Runaway servant from the snow *Fortune*, Capt. William Rowntree, lately wrecked in Chesapeake Bay. From George Brown, of Kingston, VA. (VG 5 Oct 1769).

Giles, Thomas, no age given, Runaway carpenter from the snow *Fortune*, Capt. William Rowntree, lately wrecked in Chesapeake Bay. From George Brown, of Kingston, VA. (VG 5 Oct 1769).

Gill, William, about 30, Runaway Indented Irish Servant who has the dialect, is stout made and very talkative especially when in liquor; he has an exceeding sore leg probably caused by former intemperance. From Thomas Lawson, at Neabsco Furnace, Prince William Co, VA. (VG 12 Jul 1776).

Glass, George, about 50, Runaway Servant lately transported from Liverpool on the *John & Mary*, Capt Bradley, to York River; talks broad West Country. (VG 12-19 Dec 1745).

Glass, Thomas, 45, Runaway Indented Servant who has lost a finger, ran from the ship *Chance*, Capt Campbell. From Brown, Grierson & Co, Norfolk, VA. (VG 12 Aug 1773).

Glendening, David, 35, Deserter from Camp at Maidstone, VA, born in Scotland. From Commanding Officer, Winchester, VA. (VG 27 Aug 1756).

Glover, William, about 20, 6 feet 4 inches tall, of Northampton Co, NC, Runaway Soldier Deserter from 3rd Regiment of NC Continental Troops. From Capt James Bradby. (VG 9 May 1777).

Gold, John, no age given, Runaway English Freeman with a gallows look, by trade a painter. From Edward Hill of Blandford, Prince George Co, VA. (VG 25 Jul 1766).

Good, Thomas, about 35, [*transported from Wiltshire Assizes in 1767*], Runaway English Convict Servant, born in North of England, by trade a miller. From Charles Greenbury & Henry Griffith Jr of Seneca, Frederick Co, MD.(VG 16 Jun 1768).

Goode, Thomas, about 20, Runaway English Indented Servant who carries a forged discharge, has a pleasant countenance and a clumsy way of walking. From William Settle near Fauquier Co Courthouse, VA. (VG 4 Aug 1774).

Gordon, James and wife, no ages given, who say they were born in Scotland, speak that dialect, and came over in the *Molly*, Capt Lamont, and were landed at Oxford, MD, six months ago. Suspected Runaway Servants from MD who say they are man and wife; he says he is by trade a dyer; she is of a ruddy complexion with a flippant tongue. Owner to apply to Micajah Wills, Jailer of Isle of Wight Co. VA. (VG 27 Oct 1774).

Gordon, Thomas, about 40, Suspected Runaway Servant much pitted with small pox who says he served as a gardener to Col Barnes of MD. The owner to contact Jesse Alexander, Jailer of Northampton Co, VA. (VG 20 Oct 1774).

Gothard, Joseph, no age given, Runaway Indented Servant, cooper by trade. From John Syme and John Crenshaw, Rocky Mill, Newcastle, Hanover Co, VA. (VG 21 Apr 1774).

Gounion, John, about 22, Convicted Servant, butcher, stammers much. From John Steuart on MiddleRiver, Augusta Co, VA. (VG 14 Apr 1768).

Gout, Roger, no age given, thick, short and stout, much pitted with smallpox, Runaway Sailor who deserted the ship *Hoyne* at Gosport, VA. From Inglis & Long, Williamsburg, VA. (VG 31 Jan 1771).

Grainger (Granger), Francis, 30, [sentenced by London Sessions in Apr 1773 to be transported for stealing an iron stove, for which his wife scratched his face; broke away from confinement &

sentenced for 14 years' & shipped to VA by the *Justitia* in Jan 1774], Runaway English Convict Servant born in the north of England. From Capt Finlay Gray of the said ship at Leeds Town, Rappahannock, VA. (VG 24 Mar 1774).

Gramley, Michael, about 25, Runaway Irish Servant with shaven head. From Thomas Williams of Prince William Co, VA. (VG 18 Jul 1751).

Grant, Margaret, about 20, Runaway Mulatto Servant who attends John Chambers (q.v.) as a waiting boy; she can read and write and has been in Barbados, Antigua and Philadelphia and says she was born in Carolina. From Henry James and Mordecai Gist in Baltimore, MD. (VG 5 Apr 1770).

Grant, William, no age given, Runaway Soldier Deserter from 2nd Battalion for Georgia. From Joseph Pannill, Prince Edward Courthouse, VA. (VG 27 Dec 1776).

Gray, Thomas, about 36, Runaway Servant, cabinet maker and joiner imported by indenture from London by the *Rachel*, Capt Armstrong this Summer and supposedly gone towards NC from Richmond, VA. From James Allan of Fredericksburg, VA. (VG 20 Oct 1752).

Gray, William, 19, Runaway Convict Servant with mouse-coloured hair. From Patrick Coutts, Williamsburg, VA. (VG 4 Feb 1773).

Gray, William, about 21, Runaway English Convict Servant. From Caleb Worley and Hugh Allen, Botetourt, VA. (VG 2 Dec 1773).

Green, Hugh, no age given, a tailor, Runaway Soldier Deserter from 8th Battalion in Williamsburg, VA. From James Higgin, Williamsburg. (VG 13 Dec 1776).

Green, Hugh, no age given, Runaway Soldier Deserter from 2nd Georgia Battalion who enlisted in Williamsburg, VA. From Lieut Robert Ward, Williamsburg. (VG 24 Jan 1777).

Green, Joseph, about 35, [probably the one of that name sentenced at Leicestershire Assizes in Lent 1767, reprieved to be transported for 14 years & shipped to VA in Sep 1767], Runaway English Servant pitted with smallpox who has remarkable speech and carries pen and ink. From Archibald McCall of Tappahannock, VA. (VG 18 Feb 1768).

Green, Richard, house carpenter & joiner, about 20, freckled & very talkative, went away with Scotsman James Innis (q.v). From Samuel Duval, Henrico Co, VA. (VG 14 Feb 1751).

Green, Simon, no age given, Runaway Soldier Deserter from Capt Charles Tomkies' Co of 7th Regiment and probably now in Gloucester Co, VA, where it was raised. From Reuben Lipscomb, Williamsburg, VA. (VG 24 Jan 1777).

Greton, Joseph, no age given, Servant of Richard Snowden of Anne Arundel Co, MD. In gaol at Williamsburg, VA, as runaway. (VG 30 Jun – 7 Jul 1738).

Griffin, William, about 19, Runaway Apprentice thought to be Irish but says he was born in Caroline Co, VA; in 1751 he was an overseer for Widow Thorn in Gloucester Co, VA. From John Barton near the Capitol in Williamsburg, VA. (VG 30 Jan 1752).

Griffith, William, about 30, English Convict Servant, shoemaker pitted with smallpox, probably has venereal disease, writes well. From Foushee Tebbs, near Dumfries, VA. (VG 7 Jun 1770).

Groom, Robert, 24-25, Runaway English Servant, by trade a joiner. From Thomas Fitzhugh on plantation of Rev Robert Rose of Albemarle Co deased. (VG 5 Mar 1752).

Grymes, Edward, about 24, Runaway Indented English Servant who ran from the plantation of James Pride, much pitted with smallpox, a bricklayer by trade. From William Chancey, Williamsburg, VA. (VG 18 Aug 1774).

Guier alias McGuier, Thomas, about 20, Runaway Irish Servant who has been 7 years in the country and served his time with Samuel Boush of Norfolk Borough before his present master. From Robert Waller of Norfolk Borough, VA. (VG 10 Jan 1752).

Gunn, John, 19-20, [*sentenced to transportation from London Sessions for stealing sugar & shipped by the* Justitia *to VA in Sep 1767*)], Runaway English Convict Servant, pockmarked, a plasterer by trade. From James Lyle of Burden's Lane, Augusta, VA. (VG 12 Mar 1772).

Guthry, Simon, about 40, Suspected Runaway Servant who says he came from Philadelphia. Owner to apply to John Purcell, gaoler of Richmond Co Gaol, VA. (VG 27 Sep 1770).

Gwyn, John, no age given, [*of St. Paul, Covent Garden, sentenced at Southwark Sessions in Oct 1766 & transported in Jan 1767 to VA by the* Tryal], Runaway Servant, middle-sized with a stutter that convulses his face, who served his time in St Mary's Co, MD, and is by trade a house carpenter and joiner. From William Black, Chesterfield, MD. (VG 18 Nov 1775).

Haggett, Edward, no age stated, Runaway Seaman from the *Virginian*, Capt Richard Lewis, at Littlepage's Landing, New Kent Co, VA. (VG 11-18 Apr 1745).

Haggett, James, 37. Deserter from HMS *Triton*. From Matthew Whitwell. (VG 9 May 1751).

Hagins, John, 26-27, [*The same person as accused of stealing a horse in Radnor, PA, in Aug1770?*], Supposed Runaway from PA. From Edward Hurst, Gaoler of Elizabeth City Co, VA. (VG 29 Sep 1768).

Haily, Thomas, about 36, Runaway Irish Servant. From Dr William Lynn of Fredericksburg. (VG 7-14 Aug 1746).

Halfpenny, John, 50-60, Runaway Irish Servant, pretended husbandman. From Thomas Turner, King George Co, VA. (VG 13-20 Apr 1739).

Hall, Anne, about 30, [probably wife of William Hall; a pretty fat woman, sentenced at Gloucestershire Quarter Sessions and transported in Oct 1737], Runaway Servant from Charles Oakes in King William Co, VA. (VG 28 Jul-4 Aug 1738).

Hall, Thomas, about 30, [*sentenced at Wiltshire Quarter Sessions & transported to VA by the* Justitia *in Jan 1774*], Runaway English Convict who has a long sharp nose, a scar on his left hand made by a reaping hook, pitted with smallpox, a bold talkative fellow fond of liquor. From Murthy McAboy in Fauquier Co, VA. (VG 11 Oct 1776).

Hambleton, John, no age stated. Runaway Irish Servant, pitted by small pox and with symptoms of French Disease, carpenter by trade. From Dr John Stafford. Nansemond Co, VA. (VG 28 Jul-4 Aug 1738).

Hamilton, Thomas (1773) – See Philips.

Hamilton, William, no age given, Scottish Deserter from Lieut Fleming at Suffolk, VA, born near Dumfries, Scotland and worked on the Western Branch of Elizabeth, last seen going for Edenton, NC. From Lieut Fleming at Suffolk, VA. (VG 3 Oct 1755).

Hammond, Giles, no age given, Runaway Sailor from the ship *Hoyne* at Gosport, VA. From Inglis & Long, Williamsburg, VA. (VG 31 Jan 1771).

Hammond, Thomas, 19, Deserter from Camp at Maidstone, VA, born in MD. From Commanding Officer, Winchester, VA. (VG 27 Aug 1756).

Hanan, William, Runaway English Servant, about 25, shoemaker who may make for NC. From Elias Barnaby, James French's shop in Petersburg, VA. (VG 2 May 1777).

Hansfield, Thomas, no age given, Runaway English Servant who will not acknowledge his master, now committed to Augusta Co Gaol, VA. The master to apply to George Matthews, Sheriff of Augusta. (VG 31 Oct 1771).

Hardwick, John, about 20, [*sentenced to transportation at Gloucestershire Assizes in Lent 1735 for stealing at Newent, transported to VA in Mar 1735*]; he has stinking breath and is a blacksmith. From John Aylett, King William Co, VA. (VG 8-15 Jun 1739).

Hardy, Andrew, 26-27, Runaway Soldier Deserter from 2nd Battalion recruited in Albemarle, VA, for defence of GA, thin-faced, much addicted to liquor, talkative and impertinent when intoxicated. From Lieut John Clarke, Cumberland Co, VA. (VG 7 Mar 1777).

Hargraves (Hardgraves), George, no age given, [*transported from Yorkshire Assizes in Lent 1771*], Runaway Convict Servant who has lost the upper end of one ear. From Edmund Terrill of Culpeper Co, VA. (VG 4 Jun 1772).

Harlett, Jane, no age given, Runaway Scottish Servant. From Thomas Nevett or Thomas Watkins of Cambridge, Great Choptank River, MD. (VG 15-22 Oct 1736).

Harmon, Anne, 20, Runaway English Servant, well-featured, of middle stature. From John Corries of Piscataway, Essex Co, VA. (VG 24 Sep – 1 Oct 1736).

Harn alias Harrington, James, no age given, Runaway Negro or Mulatto Servant, short, very pert and speaks above the common rank; a notorious liar and great villain, fond of spirituous liquors. From William Peachey of Richmond Co, VA. (VG 4 Nov 1763).

Harred, Hamilton, no age given, Runaway Whitehaven man. From Barthlomew Rooke, Capt of the brig *Delight* at Capt Dansie's, Williamsburg, VA. (VG 7 Nov 1754).

Harrington, James (1763) – *See* Harn.

Harris, Anne, about 30, Runaway Servant with a scarred face, big with child. From Jacob Andrew Minitree of Charles Co, Potomac, MD. (VG 7 Mar 1751).

Harris, Charles, about 18, barber by trade who was sent to King & Queen Co on business and there enquired the way to Leeds Town. From William Peak of York, VA. (VG 18 Jul 1751).

Harris, John, no age stated, Welsh Servant. From Humphry Brooke, King William Co, VA. (VG 21-28 Jul 1738).

Harris, John (1767) – *See* Homes.

Harris, William, no age given, *[probably transported from Surrey Quarter Sessions in 1769 by the Thornton]*, Suspected Convict Servant who says that he is a bricklayer by trade and he ran away from Dr William Flood; his master is Joseph Peirce in Westmoreland Co, VA, who should now apply to James Atkinson of Norfolk, VA. (VG 12 Jul 1770).

Harrison, Benjamin, no age given, about six feet tall with a large nose, Deserted from Capt Ruffin's Co. From Lieut Billey H Avery, Williamsburg, VA. (VG 10 May 1776).

Harrison, Henry, Runaway Irish Servant, no age given, shoemaker by trade with a bald head and remarkably red nose. From James Taylor of Williamsburg, VA. (VG 8 Aug 1751).

Harrison, Thomas, about 25, *[sentenced for housebreaking at Yorkshire Assizes & transported in Aug 1770]*, Servant born in the north of England, weaver by trade who writes well and is very talkative; has been seen heading towards Port Royal, VA. From Alexander Knox, Boyd's Hole, Nanjemoy, MD. (VG 3 Sep 1772).

Hart, Thomas, 23, Runaway Irish Servant with crooked little fingers, tailor by trade. From William Blyth, Fredericksburg, VA. (VG 21 Sep 1775).

Hart, William, no age given, Runaway Irish Convict Servant. From William Dames of Chester Town, MD. (VG 28 Aug-4 Sep 1746).

Harvey, John, no age given, *[Convict transported from Surrey, England, in 1732 by Caesar to VA]*, joiner. From Benjamin Berryman, High Sheriff of King George Co, VA. (VG 1-17 Jun 1737).

Haskins, Joseph, no age stated, Runaway Deserter from 7th Regiment of Virginia. From Charles Fleming of 7th Regt at Gloucester Courthouse, VA. (VG 25 May 1776).

Haslam, James, about 25, *[transported from Lancashire Assizes in Lent 1769]*, English Convict Servant. From William Renick of Augusta, VA. (VG 8 Feb 1770).

Hasset, Sarah, about 20, Runaway Irish Servant, under middle size and inclined to be fat, born in Co Limerick with a good deal of the brogue. From William Jackson Jr near Hillsborough, Orange Co, NC. (VG 17 Feb 1774).

Hatfield, James, about 23, Englishman, cooper. From David Jameson of York, VA, merchant. (VG 11 Jul 1751).

Hatfield alias Hatter, Richard, no age stated, Runaway Negro Servant who was born free but is now indented. From Samuel Lambuth of Smithfield, VA. (VG 18 May 1769).

Hatter, Edward, about 15, Runaway shoemaker. From John Aylett, King William Co, VA. (VG 8-15 Jun 1739).

Hatter, Richard (1769) – *See* Hatfield.

Hatter, William (1739) - *See* Hatton.

Hatton, Richard, 12-13, Runaway Convict Boy with a cut on the left side of his face. From George Graham of Williamsburg, VA. (VG 23 Jul 1767).

Hatton alias Hatter, William, about 20, [of Ruislip, Mddx, sentenced by Middlesex Sessions for breaking and entering Jul 1737, transported to MD Sep 1737 by the *Tryal*], shoemaker. From John Aylett, King William Co, VA. (VG 8-15 Jun 1739).

Hatton alias Jackson, William, 28-30, Runaway Convict Servant, stares at whoever speaks to him and has a scar from his mouth to his chin, by trade a stocking weaver. From Francis Phillips of Kingsbury Furnace Mine Bank near Baltimore, MD. (VG 31 Aug 1768).

Hauks, John, 23, Runaway English Indented Servant, pitted with small pox and halting in his walk. From James Campbell & Co, Norfolk, VA. (VG 15 Feb 1770).

Hawke, Richard, 55, [*sentenced at London Sessions in Dec 1774 for stealing sheep but reprieved & transported to MD for 14 years in the Saltspring in Jul 1775*], Runaway English Convict Servant of red complexion. From Thomas Aseren in Loudoun Co, VA. (VG 26 Jul 1776).

Hawkins, Benjamin, no age given, Runaway English Servant committed to Northumberland Co, VA, Jail, who says he came to this country in 1767 and served his time with Mr Harpiron of Dunmore Co, VA; he is thin faced with a down look. The owner to contact the jailer (unnamed). (VG 2 Feb 1776).

Hay, John, no age given, Runaway Scottish Indented Servant, stout made and speaks his country's brogue in a thick and chattering tone. From Ry. Randolph of Turkey Island, Henrico Co, VA. (VG 13 Apr 1769).

Hays, Elizabeth, no age given, Runaway from the snow *Fortune*, Capt. William Rowntree, lately wrecked in Chesapeake Bay. From George Brown, of Kingston, VA. (VG 5 Oct 1769).

Heden (Headen), John, no age given, [*convicted at Buckingham Assizes of stealing sheep, reprieved and transported to VA in Oct 1768 by the* Justitia], Runaway English Convict Servant with thick lips, a sore on his left leg and a scarred right knee, a blacksmith by trade. From Charles McCarty, Richmond Co, VA. (VG 5 Aug 1773).

Headford, John, middle-aged, *[convicted at Surrey Assizes and transported to VA in Jan 1738 by the Dorsetshire]*, English Servant, professes to be a cook. From Benjamin Fendall, Charles Co, MD. (VG 13-20 Jul 1739).

Heathcote, Lydia, 25, *[transported to VA for 14 years by Surrey Assizes in Jan 1774 by the Justitia]*, Runaway English Convict Servant, born in London. From Capt Finlay Gray of the said ship at Leeds Town, Rappahannock, VA. (VG 24 Mar 1774). N.B. A woman of the same name was transported from the Surrey Assizes by the *Thetis* in 1759.

Helensord alias Allinsord, Philip, about 26, Convict Servant born in Suffolk, England, who understands farming. From William Todd, King & Queen Co, VA. (VG 14 Apr 1768).

Helpen, Peter, about 30, Runaway Servant with roguish countenance, by trade a staymaker and tailor. From Joseph Simpson of Richmond Co, VA. (VG 6 Oct 1752).

Henderson, Daniel, no age given, of Staunton, Augusta, VA, Runaway Deserter Recruit raised for the Georgia Service. From Samuel Scott at Prince Edward Courthouse. (VG 27 Sep 1776).

Hendricks, George, no age given, Escaped Dutch Servant from Augusta Co Gaol, VA. From John Bowyer of said gaol. (VG 22 Dec 1768).

Henes, John, 25, Runaway Convict Servant, very lame because one leg is shorter than the other. From Peter Wise of Alexandria, Fairfax Co, VA. (VG 6 Jun 1766).

Herbert (Horbert), Thomas, about 30, *[sentenced at Middlesex Sessions in Oct 1772 for stealing a watch, reprieved and transported to MD by the Hanover Planter in May 1773]*, Runaway English Convict Servant, a silversmith. From William Alexander at Borton's Tract in Augusta, VA. (VG 18 Feb 1775).

Holland, Thomas, about 23, Runaway Deserter Soldier from 5th Battalion, Williamsburg, VA. From Gross Scruggs, Williamsburg. (VG 27 Sep 1776).

Horbert, Thomas (1775) - *See* Herbert.

Herne alias Horne, Peeling, about 24, *[sentenced at Middlesex Sessions in Jan 1774 for highway robbery, reprieved in Jul and transported to VA by the Tayloe in the same month]*, Runaway English Convict Servant who has a smooth face and a scar under his left eye. From Alexander Henderson at Bull Run in Colchester, VA. (VG 10 Nov 1774).

Hicley, Edward, about 30, Runaway English Convict Servant who stoops. From James Laderdale near Buchanan's Ferry, Augusta, VA. (VG 14 Jul 1768).

Higginson, Joseph, 21-22, *[sentenced at London Sessions in Apr 1770 for stealing a handkerchief and transported to MD by the Scarsdale in July 1770]*, Runaway English Convict Servant, a native of London who cannot read or write; he was sold to Mr Strother, then to Reuben Daniel of Orange Co and then to this advertiser; he served his time as a screwplate maker and does indifferent brass and silver work. He has been seen on his way to York. From Samuel Daniel near the (s)upper church in Middlesex Co, VA. (VG 7 Apr 1775).

Higton, Paul, young, [transported in 1768 from Nottingham Assizes], Runaway Convict Servant who is pox-marked, talks broad and is a good scholar and former schoolmaster From John Gorsuch near Baltimore, MD.(VG 1 Aug 1771).

Hill, Elijah, about 18, [sentenced at Middlesex Sessions in Oct 1771 for stealing lead and transported to VA by the Justitia in Dec 1771], Runaway Convict Servant much pitted by smallpox, writes well and is an excellent sawyer. From Randolph Spicer living near Fauquier Courthouse, VA. (VG 15 Apr 1773).

Hill, William, 19, Runaway Deserter from Halifax Regular Co now in Williamsburg. From Capt Nathaniel Cocke. (VG 20 Apr, 10 & 20 May 1776).

Hiller, John, about 33, born and bred English Servant, blacksmith by trade and much addicted to drink; has spent much time on a man of war. From Robert Stobo of Williamsburg, VA. (VG 12 Jun 1752).

Hilton, James, 45-50, Runaway English Servant with grey beard and hair who speaks bad English. From William Hughes of Hanover Co, VA. (VG 5 Mar 1752).

Hirley, Patrick, no age given, Convict Servant born in Ireland, a little pitted by smallpox and very lame from a broken thigh. From Benjamin Welsh of Bush River Furnace, South River, MD. (VG 24 Dec 1767).

Hitchings, James, no age given, Runaway sailor from the snow *Fortune*, Capt. William Rowntree, lately wrecked in Chesapeake Bay. From George Brown, of Kingston, VA. (VG 5 Oct 1769).

Hobbs, James, 22 or 23, [sentenced at Middlesex Sessions in Jul 1731 for stealing two pairs of shoes, transported in Sep 1731 and landed in VA in 1732 from the *Smith*], ship carpenter lately living at Appomattox, VA. From William Ruff near Gray's Creek opposite James Town, VA. (VG 21-28 Sep 1739).

Hobday, Richard, about 17, Runaway Apprentice Lad. From Humphrey Harwood, Williamsburg, VA. (VG 5 Sep 1771).

Hobday alias Dobson, Robert, no age given, Runaway Servant, by trade a wheelwright who has two nipples on his left breast. From William Trebell of Williamsburg, VA. (VG 4 Nov 1763).

Hobdy, Edmund, about 19, Runaway apprentice tailor who endeavours to pass for a freeman. From Francis Durfey, Charles City, VA. (VG 21 Mar 1771).

Hogan, James, no age stated, Runaway Servant who served his time with Thomas Riggs of Frederick Co, MD, and stole goods of Mary Pearce of Fairfax Co, VA. From Peter Pearce, Pinkney, Williamsburg, VA. (VG 12 Jan 1775).

Hoggart, Samuel, 19, tailor. From Thomas Wilson of Norfolk Borough, VA. (VG 31 Jan 1751; from Lewis Burwell of Norfolk Borough. (VG 28 Feb 1751).

Hollingshaw alias Holshaw, Michael, no age stated, runaway from Patapsco Ironworks in MD, Dutch servant speaking bad English, seen between Patapsco and Annapolis, MD. From Charles Carroll & Co. (VG 30 Jul 1752).

Holmes alias Commodore, John, no age given, Irish Servant, cooper, served as soldier under Gen Braddock, remarkable reprobate when drunk. From Robert Rutherford of Winchester, VA. (VG 14 Jan & 14 Jun 1770).

Holmes, Samuel, no age given, Runaway Servant who stammers much and is bow-legged with a great scar on one leg caused by ulcers, by trade a tailor. From William Taite of Northumberland, VA. (VG 4 Apr 1766).

Homes, Samuel alias Harris, John, no age given, (the same as above), Runaway Servant with a yellow scar on the right cheek and a large yellow spot on his left knee, a tailor. From William Taite of Northumberland Co, VA. (VG 26 Mar 1767).

Holmes, William, about 45 Runaway recruit from King William Co, mulatto about 6 feet tall. From John Russel of King William Co. (VG 28 Feb 1755).Runaway Convict Servant

Holshaw, Michael (1752) - See Hollingshaw.

Hooper, Richard, no age given, Suspected Deserter from Deep Spring Camp, VA, of 6th Virginia Regiment. Warning from Capt James Johnson of said Regt. (VG 30 Aug 1776).

Horne, Peeling (1774) – See Herne.

Horn alias Cole, Richard, 25, Runaway Servant, pretended smith, short, pert, impudent and pox-ridden. From Robert Vaulx, Westmoreland Co, Potomac, VA. (VG 2 May 1751).

How, Richard (1745) – See Butler, Thomas.

Howard, Corker, no age given, of Gloucester Co, VA, Runaway Soldier Deserter believed to be in Robin's Neck. From William Pierce Jr, Williamsburg, VA. (VG 28 Mar 1777).

Howard alias Johnson, John, about 30, Runaway Irish Servant, carpenter and joiner by trade, formerly belonging to Thomas Whiting deceased of Gloucester Co, VA. From Joseph Cocke of Williamsburg, VA. (VG 8-15 May 1746).

Howard, John, no age given, of Gloucester Co, VA, Runaway Soldier Deserter believed to be in Robin's Neck. From William Pierce Jr, Williamsburg, VA. (VG 28 Mar 1777).

Howard Sarah (1752) – See Knox.

How(e), James, about 40, [*sentenced at London Sessions 27 Feb 1745 for stealing a wig from a shop & transported to VA by the Justitia in May 1745*], Runaway English Convict Servant, bald and pox-ridden. From Maj Andrew Campbell of Frederick Co, VA. (VG 20-27 Mar 1746).

Howell, Henry, about 20, ruddy complexion, of Edgecombe Co, NC, Runaway Soldier Deserter from 3rd Regiment of NC Continental Troops. From Capt James Bradby. (VG 9 May 1777).

Howell, Samuel, about 28, Mulatto Servant bound until he is 31, brother of Simon Howell. From Wade Netherland of Cumberland Co, VA. (VG 16 Aug 1770).

Howell, Simon, about 25, Mulatto Servant bound until he is 31, brother of Samuel Howell. From Wade Netherland of Cumberland Co, VA. (VG 16 Aug 1770).

Hoy, Thomas, about 41, Runaway Irish Servant with a broken little finger, scars on an eye and head, given to strong drink and plays well on the violin when in liquor; pretends to teach dancing. From Tsb De Graffenreid, Prince George Co, VA. (VG 19-26 Sep 1745).

Hudson, Charles, no age given, Suspected Deserter from Deep Spring Camp, VA, of 6th Virginia Regiment. Warning from Capt James Johnson of said Regt. (VG 30 Aug 1776).

Hudson, John, about 35, Runaway Seaman Deserter from the galley *Hero* where he acted for some time as boatswain's mate; he may try to get near Pittsburg where he has land. From George Muter, Portsmouth, VA. (VG 20 Sep 1776).

Hudson, William, about 19, apprentice tailor who plays the violin well. From Richard Phillips, near Bowler's Ferry, Essex, VA. (VG 31 Oct 1771).

Hughes, Billy alias Lester, Thomas, Irish Convict Servant & notorious villain convicted for robbery in Louisa Co, VA, in December 1750 under the name of Lester. From Thomas Dansie of King William Co, VA. (VG 9 May 1751).

Hughs, John, middle-aged, Runaway Irish Servant recently arrived in the country, calls himself a farmer and belongs to Dr Ephraim Howard, son of Henry Howard. (VG 26 Jul 1770).

Hulse, William, about 20, not quick of apprehension. From Robert Yates of St Mary's Co, MD. (VG 28 Jul – 4 Aug 1738).

Humphreys, Daniel, Runaway Indented Welsh Servant, about 26, a tailor by trade, halts exceedingly in his walk and ran from the south side of the Capitol, Williamsburg, VA. From Samuel Harris of Williamsburg. (VG 15 Nov 1776).

Humphrey, David, no age stated, Runaway Seaman from the *Virginian*, Capt Richard Lewis, at Littlepage's Landing, New Kent Co, VA. (VG 11-18 Apr 1745).

Hundley, Matthew, no age given, Deserter from Capt Reuben Lipscomb's Co in Amelia Co, VA. Reward offered by Lieut Tarpley White, Williamsburg, Va. (VG 28 Mar 1777).

Hunt, George, no age given, Runaway Servant, lusty, hard and tall, by trade a caulker, gone with a strolling woman towards the Northern Neck. From William Meredith of Williamsburg, VA. (VG 20 Oct 1752).

Hunt alias Williams, Mary, no age given, Servant born in England. From Anthony Walke of Petersburg, VA, merchant. (VG 5 Jun 1752).

Hunter, John, no age given, Runaway Indented English Servant, born in London, speaks very quick and has a comical, sly and squinting look. From Elkanah Deane in Williamsburg, VA. (VJ 23 Feb 1775).

Hunter, John, about 25, Runaway English Servant, a pretty good scholar likely to pass for a schoolmaster. From Francis Thomas near Sugarloaf Mountain, Frederick Co, MD. (VG 13 Oct 1775).

Hurley, John (1767) - See Knowles.

Hurst, Henry, Runaway Convict Servant, no age given, stammers much when frightened, a little pitted with smallpox. From Thomas Robins in Orange Co, VA. (VG 28 Jul 1774).

Hutchinson, John, no age given, Runaway English Servant, stout, born in Yorkshire, a blacksmith by trade, *(transported from Yorkshire Assizes in Lent 1771)*. From Thomas Pollard, Lancaster Co, VA. (VG 24 Sep & 26 Nov 1772).

Hynds, Luke, no age given, Runaway Irish Servant who will not tell his master's name and talks very quick. The owner to apply to John Nevill of Frederick Co Gaol. (VG 5 Sep 1771).

Ingles, Andrew, no age given, Runaway Scottish Indented Servant swarthy and long-featured with a scab over his right eye, fond of liquor and talks his country's dialect, by trade a baker. From James Kirk of Alexandria, VA. (VG 17 Jun 1775).

Ingram, Joseph, about 28, Runaway Irish Convict Servant with a sly look who sings and understands farming well. From Henry Coleman in Spotsylvania Co, VA. (VG 3 Aug 1775).

Innis, James, Scotsman, about 24, went away with Richard Green (q.v.). From Samuel Duval, Henrico Co, VA. (VG 14 Feb 1751).

Innes, William, about 20, Runaway Irish Servant who talks the brogue very much and may pass for a seaman. From Alexander Bissitt of Petersburg, VA. (VG 21 Jul 1768).

Irwin, Francis, no age given, Runaway Irish Convict Servant, stout with a remarkably hoarse voice, by trade a blacksmith. From Samuel Canby, Loudoun Co, VA. (VG 8 Jun 1775).

Jackson, Anthony, about 20, [*transported to MD from Surrey Assizes by the* Thornton *in May 1770*], Runaway English Convict Servant, born in Yorkshire and is a little stooped in the shoulders. From John Hood Sr and John Hood Jr of Elk Ridge, Anne Arundel Co, MD. (VG 27 Sep 1770).

Jackson, Thomas, about 30, Runaway Indented Servant, coachman by trade. From John Syme and John Crenshaw, Rocky Mill, Newcastle, Hanover Co, VA. (VG 21 Apr 1774).

Jackson, William, about 27, Runaway Servant with a scar on his lip. From William Jenkins of Frederick Co, VA. (VG 31 May 1770).

Jackson, William (1768) *See* Hatton.

Jakins, William, 24, Runaway Servant just imported in the *Wilcox*, a ploughman. From Peter Randolph of Williamsburg. (VG 16 May 1755).

Jamieson, Alexander, no age given, Runaway Scottish Servant, by trade a weaver, complicit in the murder of Thomas Horton, skipper of a small schooner returning from Norfolk, VA. From David Galloway of Northumberland C, VA. (VG 19-26 Sep 1745).

Jardine, John, no age given, Runaway English Convict who was born in Cumberland and speaks the dialect, thick, well set, round shouldered and pitted with smallpox. From John Carlyle, Alexandria, VA. (VG 6 Aug 1772).

Jefferson, John, about 20, Runaway English Convict Servant (*awaiting transportation from Northumberland Assizes in Summer 1765*), a weaver. From Samuel McDowell of Burden's Lane, Augusta, VA. (VG 12 Mar 1772).

Jenkings, John, about 28, Runaway English Convict Servant, cooper by trade, a little stooped, transported by the *Dorsetshire* from Middlesex Assizes in 1739. From George Turberville of Westmoreland Co, VA. (VG 13-20 Jul 1739).

Jenkins, William, about 45, Runaway English Convict Servant who has been aboard several of HM ships, by trade a cabinet maker. From Thomas Miller of Fredericksburg, VA. (VG 25 Jun 1772).

Johns, Daniel, 18-19, Runaway Sailor Lad from the ship *Hoyne* at Gosport, VA. From Inglis & Long, Williansburg, VA. (VG 31 Jan 1771).

Johnson, Henry, no age given, Runaway English Convict Servant who has a large scar on his head, talks much in a hoarse and coarse voice, and is quarrelsome when drunk. From Robert Phillips at Fredericksburg, VA. (VG 28 Jan 1768).

Johnson, James (1745). *See* Gibson.

Johnson, John (1746) – *See* Howard.

Johnson, John, no age given, runaway ploughman. From Armistead Churchill, Middlesex Co, VA. (VG 12 Jun 1752).

Johnson, John, about 22, Runaway Servant, slim and watery-eyed, who is believed to have taken a negro slave. From John Holt, Williamsburg, VA. (VG 12 Jan 1775).

Johnson, Samuel (1773) - *See* Johnson.

Johnson, William, Runaway English Convict Servant (*perhaps the one of this name transported from Middlesex Sessions for life by the* Justitia *in Oct 1768*), thin visage, small legs, speaks briskly and a reasonably good scholar, a plasterer by trade. From James Lyle of Burden's Land, Augusta, VA. (VG 12 Mar 1772).

Johnston, John, about 23, Runaway Seaman born in Scotland, about 6 feet tall, pitted with smallpox, from the *Encouragement* of London lying at West Point, VA. From Alexander Douglas of the said ship. (VG 10 Apr 1752).

Johnston (Johnson), Samuel, no age given, [*transported to VA from Middlesex Sessions by the* Tayloe *in 1772 for stealing butter*], Runaway English Servant who has stooped shoulders, when in liquor fond of singing and very talkative; pretends to be well acquainted with the City of London and to have been in the East Indies. From John Draper, Williamsburg, VA. (VG 11 Nov 1773).

Johnston, William, 25, Runaway Indentured Servant, ruddy complexion, speaks good English, lately from the ship; was in the country before trading as a painter, limner and glazier. From John Grattan on the great road near Abbotstown, York Co, PA. (VG 4 Feb 1768).

Johnston, William, 17-18, Runaway Apprentice Lad born in or near Williamsburg, VA, knock-kneed and a little pitted with smallpox who was bound to a staymaker in Surry Co, VA. From James Belches of the brig *Innermay* lying at Brandon, VA. (VG 21 Jan 1775).

Joiner, Matthew, about 20, stout and bow-legged, of Edgecombe Co, NC, Runaway Soldier Deserter from 3rd Regiment of NC Continental Troops. From Capt James Bradby. (VG 9 May 1777).

Jolley, Joseph, no age given, Runaway Deserter Soldier of 5th Battalion at College Camp, Williamsburg, stout with stooped shoulders, addicted to liquor and when drunk is troublesome; he may head for Henrico Co where he has family. From John Pleasants, Williamsburg. (VG 20 Sep 1776).

Jones, Benjamin, no age given, dark and has a black beard, Runaway Soldier Deserter from 2nd Virginia Regiment in NJ and probably lurking about Baltimore. From Col Alexander Spotswood of said Regiment. (VG 5 Sep 1777).

Jones, David, about 40, [*convicted Oct 1772 at Middlesex Sessions for stealing a handkerchief and transported to VA by the* Justitia *in Jan 1773*], Runaway Welsh Convict Servant, blind in the right eye. From Caleb Worley and Hugh Allen, Botetourt, VA. (VG 2 Dec 1773).

Jones, Edward, no age given, Suspected Runaway English Servant who says he belongs to Capt Nathaniel Chew of the ship *Hannah* lying in Patuxent River, MD, and ran after her arrival. From Lewis Neill of Frederick Co Gaol, MD. (VG 17 Oct 1751).

Jones, James, no age given, Welsh Servant Runaway, nearly six feet high, dark and swarthy. From Daniel & Menoah Singleton, Orange Co, VA. (VG Supp 22 July 1773).

Jones, James, no age given, Suspected Deserter from Deep Spring Camp, VA, of 6th Virginia Regiment. Warning from Capt James Johnson of said Regt. (VG 30 Aug 1776).

Jones, John, about 40, Runaway Welsh Servant with a wen the size of an egg on the back of his hand. From John Danby, upper parish of Nansemond Co, VA. (VG 13-20 Apr 1739).

Jones, John, about 35, Runaway English Convict Servant who has been a sailor and who altered his name at Fredericksburg, VA; he is a very good scholar. From Andrew Burd of Augusta, VA. (VG 26 Feb 1767).

Jones, John, about 36, Runaway English Convict Servant born in Liverpool but can speak Welsh, pitted with smallpox, round-shouldered with a stooped walk and a scar on his left leg caused by a wound received at sea. From Patrick Lockhart in Botetourt, VA. (VG 26 May & 2 Jun 1774).

Jones, Major, no age given, Deserter from Capt John Blair's Co of 9th Virginia Regiment when under marching orders. From Lieut Thomas Overton, Williamsburg, VA. (VG 11 Jul 1777).

Jones, Philip, about 22, supposedly gone towards Brunswick Co, VA. From Emory Hughes, James City Co, VA. (VG 24 Jan 1751).

Jones, Richard, no age given, Runaway Soldier Deserter from 3rd Regiment of NC enlisted in Bute Co, NC, short and dark. From Lieut William Linton. (VG 9 May 1777).

Jones, Samuel, no age given, Runaway Apprentice who left to see his mother in Warwick Co and did not return. From Matthew Langstone, Cumberland Co, VA. (VG 29 Nov 1776).

Jones, Thomas, no age stated, Runaway Seaman from the *Virginian*, Capt Richard Lewis, at Littlepage's Landing, New Kent Co, VA. (VG 11-18 Apr 1745).

Jones, Thomas, no age stated, [*transported for 14 years from Leicester Assizes for highway robbery in 1746 by the ship Laura*], Runaway English Convict Servant, shoemaker by trade, brought in by Capt Gracie to Rappahannock, VA. From Matthew Wellman of Hanover Co, VA. (VG 11-18 Sep 1746).

Jones, Thomas, no age stated, Welsh Servant Runaway, about 6 feet tall, speaks several languages and writes well. From James Pattie of Port Royal, Caroline Co, VA. (VG 7 Jan 1768).

Jones, Thomas, about 20, Runaway Convict Servant with a down look. From Charles G Griffith & Henry Griffith Jr of Seneca, Frederick Co, MD.(VG 16 Jun 1768).

Jones, William, about 30, Welshman employed in plantation work. From Randall Allen, Williamsburg, VA. (VG 15-22 Jun 1739).

Jones, William, no age given, Runaway Soldier Deserter of 6th Virginia Battalion. From the sloop *Susanna* at Leeds Town, VA. From Ensign Harden Perkins, Williamsburg, VA. (VG 18 Oct 1776).

Jones, William, no age stated, claims he was born in West of England and speaks the dialect but believed to be a deserter from a VA regiment; he was much troubled with fever and ague. From Frederick Smith of north fork of Roanoke, Botetourt Co, VA. (VG 25 Oct 1776).

Jordan, James, about 35, [*reprieved Apr 1773 at Wiltshire Assizes to be transported to VA*], Runaway Scottish Servant, lame in one foot and cannot wear a normal shoe, has a cut across his nose and forehead, has been in the Army and loves liquor. From Andrew Cubbin of Petersburg, VA. (VG 27 Apr 1769).

Kating, Arthur, 34-40, Runaway Indentured Servant, much freckled with a down look who crossed James River to Hog Island and was seen since on the road to Smithfield, VA. From Humphrey Harwood of Williamsburg, VA. (VG 21 Dec 1769).

Keating, John, no age given, [*transported for 14 years from Kent Assizes by the* Tryal *in 1752*], Runaway English Convict Servant, an old soldier. From Robert Stevenson near the Stone Meeting House, Augusta Co, VA. (VG 11 Aug 1768).

Keays alias Murphy, James, Irish Convict joiner. From Charles Neilson of Prince George Co, VA.; then from HMS *Triton* in Norfolk, VA, after his capture in Carolina. (VG 4 Apr 1751; 8 Aug 1751).

Keef, John, no aged given, a painter who has lived in Williamsburg, VA, for some months having come hither in 1750 on the *Dutchess of Queensbury* as an indentured servant; he is suspected of stealing money bills. (VG 15 May 1752).

Keeling, Andrew, alias Fitzjarrel, Morris. [*sentenced at Middlesex Sessions in Jun 1770 for breaking and entering & transported to MD in Jul 1770 by the Scarsdale*], Runaway Irish Convict Servant, much pitted with smallpox, has remarkably thick legs and has lost his left eye, a joiner by trade. From Charles McCarty, Richmond Co, VA. (VG 5 Aug 1773).

Keeves, Joseph, about 22, Convict Servant Runaway, lately sick. Supposedly gone to NC. From Sampson & George Matthews, Richmond, VA. (VG 12 Aug 1773).

Kelly, Andrew, no age given, Runaway Irish Servant, very fond of liquor which makes him talkative, inclined to be fat, may attempt to go to British troops. From James Parsons in Alexandria, VA. (VG 20 Sep 1776). Now confined by Williamsburg Gaoler Peter Pelham. (VG 27 Sep 1776).

Kelly, Bryan, no age given, Runaway Irish Convict Servant, talks thick upon the brogue, professes towo be a gardener by trade, much pox ridden. From Daniel Hornby, Williamsburg, VA. (VG 26 Aug-2 Sep 1737).

Kelly, Emanuel, no age given, country born, a wheelwright by trade, Runaway Soldier Deserter from 2nd Georgia Battalion. From Capt William Smith, Williamsburg, VA. (VG 6 Dec 1776).

Kelly alias Kemble, Emanuel, no age given, Runaway Soldier Deserter from 15th Continental Battalion, thought to be on Potomac River. From Capt William Grimes, Williamsburg, VA. (VG 28 Mar 1777).

Kelly, Michael and Margaret, no ages given, Runaway Irish Servants who are man and wife both speaking Irish but not known to speak English. From William Hayth on Great Falling River, Bedford Co, VA. (VG 16 May 1771).

Kelly, Thomas, no age given, no age given. Deserter from Capt Smith's Co of 2nd Georgia Battalion who claimed to have been a prisoner of the Indians. From Lieut Alexander Baugh of Cumberland Courthouse, VA. (VG 21 Feb 1777).

Kemble, Emanuel (1777) – See Kelly.

Kemp, James, no age given, [*perhaps the one of that name who was sentenced and reprieved for 14 years' transportation by Cheshire Assizes in Lent 1775*], Runaway Soldier Deserter from 2nd Battalion for Georgia. From Joseph Pannill, Prince Edward Courthouse, VA. (VG 27 Dec 1776).

Kennedy, John, about 26, Runaway Irish Servant who ran from the ship *Catherine*, Capt Thomas Patton, long-faced, who pretends to have served in an English Regiment and may attempt to pass as a freeman. From North & Sands, Norfolk, VA. (VG 23 Feb 1775).

Kenwell, Charles, no age given, Runaway English Convict Servant with a dark complexion almost like a mulatto. From William Ficklin of King George Co, VA. (VG 11-18 Sep 1746).

Kerr, Thomas, no age given, Runaway Convict Servant, no age given. From John Botkin of Augusta, VA. (VG 22 Dec 1768).

Keyon, Joseph, no age stated, Runaway Irish Servant, short and pox-ridden. From John Canaday of Fairfax Co, VA. (VG 24-31 Jul 1746).

Kibble (Keeble), Richard, young fellow, [*transported from Surrey Assizes to VA by the* Forward *in 1737 for stealing shoes and from Middlesex Sessions by the same ship in 1739*], carpenter and joiner by trade. Runaway from Capt McCarty's plantation at Pope's Creek, Westmoreland Co, VA. From Augustine Washington, Prince William Co, VA. (VG 2-9 Jun 1738); from William Walker of Westmoreland Co. (29 Jun-6 Jul 1739).

Kinchley (Kinchler), Peter, no age given, [*sentenced at Middlesex Sessions for stealing lead Sep & transported to VA in Dec 1770 by the* Justitia], Runaway Irish Servant who says he belongs to Robert Beedles of Orange Co. The master to apply to George Mathews, Sheriff of Augusta. (VG 31 Oct 1771).

Kindrick, William, no age given, Runaway Apprentice, bricklayer. From James Geddy of King William Co Courthouse (VG 2 Apr 1767).

King, John, about 25, [*perhaps the one of that name sentenced at Kent Assizes in Lent 1749 and transported to MD in May 1749 by the* Lichfield], Runaway Servant who is supposed to practise physic and surgery but understands neither. From Thomas Willis of Isle of Wight Co, VA. (VG 28 Feb 1751).

King, Thomas, about 30, Indented Servant born in England and imported in March 1774 by the *Chance,* Capt. Campbell stout and well-set, a bricklayer. From Richard Sprigg, Williamsburg, VA. (VG 7 Jun 1774).

Kitchinman, William, no age given [*convicted at Middlesex Sessions in Sep 1737 for stealing printed calico & transported to VA by the* Dorsetshire *in Jan 1738*], Runaway English Convict. From Col Henry Willis of Fredericksburg, Spotsylvania Co, VA. (VG 2-9 Mar 1739).

Kittler, John Charles, Runaway Dutch Servant, about 23, a breeches maker who may pass for a tailor, speaks good French but bad English. From Casper Herriter, Suffolk Co, VA. (VG 7 & 8 Jun 1776).

Knight, Peter, no age given, [*sentenced to transportation at West Kent Quarter Sessions in Jan & transported to VA in Apr 1772 on the* Thornton], Runaway English Convict Servant of very dark complexion John Kidd, Commander of the *Thornton* lying short and well made with sore legs. From Capt Kidd at Leeds Town, VA. (VG 23 Jul 1772).

Knowles alias Hurley, John, no age given, Runaway Irish Servant marked with smallpox, blacksmith by trade but passes for a sailor or waterman. From Samuel Stevens of Talbot Co, MD. (VG 3 Sep 1767).

Knox alias Howard alias Wilson, Sarah, [*sentenced to transportation at Cumberland Assizes Summer 1750 Session*],Runaway Convict Servant with a short nose who says she was born in Yorkshire, talks broad, and lost her husband at the Battle of Culloden; a deceitful woman and great liar. From David

Currier of Lancaster Co, VA. (VG 3 Jul 1752). Also listed in 1753 as "dancing mistress who was born in Yorkshire, fought at Culloden and imported by the *Duke of Cumberland* from Whitehaven (Cumberland)."

Kuo, Thomas, about 35, Suspected Runaway English Servant, pitted with smallpox, short straight black hair. From William Lane gaoler of Williamsburg, VA. (VG 11 Oct 1770)

Lamb, John, about 25, Indentured Servant given to drink, a tailor lately from the ship. From John Grattan of the great road near Abbottstown, York Co, Pa. (VG 4 Feb 1768).

Lamb, John, about 22, bred in Orange Co near Col Burnley's, enlisted by Lieut Garland Burnley, Runaway Deserter from Capt Spencer's Co of Regulars before they left Orange Co, VA. From Joseph Spencer, Williamsburg Headquarters. (VG 5 Jul 1776).

Lancaster, John, 25, Deserter from 4th Virginia Battalion in Portsmouth, VA, born in Isle of Wight Co who has a red beard and is likely to go to NC with which he is acquainted. From Capt Archibald Smith, Williamsburg. (VG 20 Sep 1776).

Lacy, Hugh, no age stated, Runaway Irish Servant, a young man recently arrived in the country and belonging to Dr Ephraim Howard, son of Henry Howard. From Charles Hammond. (VG 26 Jul 1770).

Lane, Michael, no age given, Runaway Servant lately from Ireland. From Samuel Canby, Loudoun Co, VA. (VG 8 Jun 1775).

Lane, Nathaniel, 21, a sober serious fellow with a florid complexion and downcast look who talks very little, Runaway Soldier who deserted from a Company of Continental Regulars. From Thomas Massie, Williamsburg, VA, Headquarters. (VG 17 May 1776).

Lange, William, middle-aged, Runaway Seaman born in Scotland, pitted with smallpox, from the *Encouragement* of London lying at West Point, VA. From Alexander Douglas of the said ship. (VG 10 Apr 1752).

Langham, James – *See* Field, Thomas.

Lankins, John, no age given, Runaway Servant, a lusty and swarthy fellow. From Samuel Thornbery, John Shippey and William Beavars of Loudoun Co, VA. (VG 7 Sep 1769).

Lawrence, Edward, no age given, Runaway plasterer from the snow *Fortune*, Capt. William Rowntree, lately wrecked in Chesapeake Bay. From George Brown, of Kingston, VA. (VG 5 Oct 1769).

Lawson, Ralph, 22, [*transported from Middlesex Quarter Sessions in Jan 1774 by the* Justitia], Runaway English Convict, Servant born in London, a fresh scar on his nose. From Capt Finlay Gray of said ship at Leeds Town, Rappahannock, VA. (VG 24 Mar 1774).

Layne, William (1745) – *See* Owl, John.

Leadbeater alias Libiter, John of Manchester, about 35, [*transported from Lancashire Quarter Sessions in Oct 1769*)], Runaway English Convict Servant of Manchester, Lancsa, who has a broad round face pitted with smallpox. From James Duncanson, Fredericksburg, VA. (VG 21 Jun 1770).

Leaker, James, about 23, Runaway Indented English Servant born in Powley, Somerset, yeoman with a remarkable sore leg. From Samuel Garlick of King William Co., VA. (VG 12 Mar 1767).

Lee, Edward, 27-28, Runaway Irish Soldier Deserter who served his time in Loudoun Co, VA. From Samuel Arell, Alexandria, VA. (VG 27 Dec 1776).

Lee, James, about 35, [*transported in 1766 from Lancashire Quarter Sessions*], Runaway English Convict Servant born near Manchester, Lancashire, who speaks the dialect to perfection, much pitted with smallpox, round-shouldered, a tolerable practical farmer and excellent ploughman believed to have left Fredericksburg last April. From Jonathan Boucher living near Fredericksburg, VA. (VG 11 May & 1 Jun 1769).

Lee, John, alias Falmouth, John, no age stated, joiner, Irish Papist. From Charles Carter, King George Co, VA. (VG 4-11 Mar 1737).

Lee, John, of Bedford, VA, no age given. Deserter from Capt Smith's Co of 2nd Georgia Battalion. From Lieut Alexander Baugh of Cumberland Courthouse, VA. (VG 21 Feb 1777).

Lee, Thomas, 40-50, [sentenced at Gloucester Assizes in Lent 1736 for stealing at Standish, Glos, reprieved Summer 1736 to be transported for 14 years, shipped in Oct 1737], tall and thin, Convict Runaway much disfigured by smallpox who has lost a finger, a joiner by trade. From John Lewis of Gloucester Co, VA. (VG 21-28 Apr 1738).

Lee, William, no age given, Runaway English Servant, marked with smallpox and has a remarkably long nose, speaks thick and is impudent. From John Purvis, Williamsburg, VA. (VG 17 Jun 1775).

Leighton, James, about 20, [*sentenced at Huntingdon Assizes in Lent 1775 to be transported for stealing iron in Houghton cum Wyton*], Runaway English Convict born in Cambridgeshire, strong and clumsy made, swarthy with thick lips. From Isaac Zane, Marlborough Ironworks, Frederick Co, VA. (VG 23 Nov 1775).

Lennon, Andrew, about 19, Runaway English Apprentice Lad who ran from on board the snow *St Bees*, Capt Benjamin Jackson. From Henry Fleming, Norfolk, VA. (VG 15 Jun 1775).

Lester, Thomas (1751) – *See* Hughes, Billy.

Lewellin, Christopher, 21-22, Servant blacksmith pitted with smallpox, imported by the ship *Rachael* in 1750. From WilliamTaliaferro of King & Queen Co, VA. (VG 21 Aug 1752).

Lewellin, Elizabeth, about 25, Runaway Welsh Convict Servant [sentenced at Middlesex Sessions Jul 1773 for stealing a silk purse, transported to VA from Middlesex Sessions in Jul 1773 by the *Tayloe*], fresh and lusty with a remarkable scar on her throat. From Patrick Lockhart in Botetourt, VA. (VG 26 May 1774).

Lewis, Evan, about 35, Runaway Indentured Welsh Servant pitted with smallpox, a house joiner by trade, imported in the ship *Becky*, Capt Buchanan, in 1751. From Robert Waller of Norfolk Borough, VA. (VG 10 Jan 1752).

Lewis, Isaac, no age given, Suspected Runaway Servant, by trade a wagon maker, committed to Essex Co Jail, VA, who says he is native of PA. Owner to contact jailer James Emerson. (VG 17 Nov 1775).

Lewis, John, about 18, Runaway Servant Lad, pretended sailor. From John Carter of Williamsburg, VA. (VG 30 May-6 Jun 1745).

Lewis, John, about 25, lately pitted with smallpox, ran from the *Industrious Bee* at Sandy Point, VA. From Henry Pascal of the said vessel. (VG 5 Jun 1752).

Lewis, Richard, 35, Runaway English Soldier Deserter from 2nd Virginia Regiment in NJ, much marked with smallpox, he formerly lived in Loudoun Co, VA. From Col Alexander Spotswood of said Regiment. (VG 5 Sep 1777).

Libiter, John – *See* Leadbeater.

Liddle, Adam, 18-20, Runaway Scottish Seaman Deserter from the sloop *Scorpion*. From Wright Westcott of said vessel. (VG 4 Oct 1776).

Linch, James, 26, Deserter from Camp at Maidstone, VA, born in Ireland. From Commanding Officer, Winchester, VA. (VG 27 Aug 1756).

Liney, John, no age given, Runaway Servant, shoemaker by trade with a bald head and remarkably red nose. From William Willcock of Williamsburg, VA. (VG 8 Aug 1751).

Linley, John, about 27, Convict Servant born in Yorkshire, ploughman. From Francis Tomkies of Gloucester Co, VA. (VG 11 Apr 1755).

Lively, William, about 23, Runaway Mulatto Servant, square-made with a large upper lip and short chin. From Lewis Boaten of Roberson Fork, Culpeper Co, VA. (VG 15 Jul 1773).

Lloyd, Joseph, about 21, [transported from Middlesex Quarter Sessions by the ship *Thornton* in April 1772; indicted in Jan 1775 of returning before expiration of his sentence, reprieved because of an error in his indictment but transported again to MD for 14 years in Jul 1775 by the *Saltspring*], Runaway English Convict Servant, house carpenter and joiner who understands little of his business, has had the smallpox favourably. From Rawleigh Dowman, Morattico, Lancaster Co, VA. (VG 4 Nov & 30 Dec 1773).

Long, Thomas, Runaway Scottish Rebel, no age stated. From Jacob Andrew Minitree, Charles Co, Potomac, MD. (VG 7 Mar 1751).

Loveday, Joseph, about 23, [*transported from London Sessions in Dec 1772 to VA on the* Justitia], Runaway English Convict Servant from the West of England, with a lame leg red beard and squeaky voice who ran at Leeds Town, VA. From Thomas Hodge or Thomas Lawson at Neabsco Furnace, Prince William Co, VA. (VG 9 Apr 1772, 24 Jun & 8 Jul 1773).

Lucas, William, no age given. Deserter from Capt Nathaniel Cocke's Co of 7th Virginia Regiment. From Lieut Tarpley White, Williamsburg, VA. (VG 28 Mar 1777).

Lupton, Edward, 25, Runaway Irish Convict, shoemaker, slender and with a thin visage, very saucy and impertinent, formerly in possession of John Hook, merchant in Bedford NC who sold him to merchants Chambers & Montgomery in Salisbury NC from whom he fled. Owner to approach Peter Pelham, Jailer of Williamsburg, VA. (VG 27 Oct 1774).

Luscombe, William, 17-18, Runaway Servant Boy. From Roger North in Staunton, VA. (VG 26 May 1775).

Lynn, Robert, 26, Deserter from Capt Polson's Co in Col Dunbar's Regiment, born in Londonderry and resident in MD, labourer. From General Braddock at Winchester, VA. (VG 9 May 1755).

Mace, Henry, no age given, Runaway Private Soldier Deserter from 2nd Virginia Regiment in NJ. From Col Alexander Spotswood of said Regiment. (VG 5 Sep 1777).

Macey, John, about 24, [*sentenced Apr 1738 in unknown court*], Runaway Convict Servant, tailor, well-set, white looking fellow, supposedly gone towards Goochland. From William Wyatt, Williamsburg, VA, in Apr 1738. (VG 25 Aug – 8 Sep 1738).

Macknell, William, Runaway Indented Servant of Whitehaven, about 19, of low stature. From William Binsley, Master of the snow *Castle* lying at York Town, VA. (VG 19 May 1774).

Mackue, John, no age given, Irish Servant, blacksmith by trade. From John Bushrode of Westmoreland Co, VA. (1-17 Aug 1739).

Macmillion, Philip, about 23, [*sentenced at London Sessions Oct, sentenced & transported to VA Nov 1728 by the* Forward, *landed at Rappahannock, VA, Jun 1729*], Runaway from Wicomico, Northumberland Co, VA, short, professes to be a tailor, makes petticoats, and to have been a planter. From Philip Smith of Northumberland Co. (VG 13-20 Jan 1738).

MacNeal, John, middle-aged, Runaway from Wicomico, Northumberland Co, VA, plantation overseer, tall, well set and pox-ridden; also professes to be a ploughman and coachman; he has dark curling Hair with a wen on his gum the size of a small nut. From Philip Smith of Northumberland Co. (VG 13-20 Jan 1738).

McKey (Mackey), George, no age given, [*sentenced at London Sessions in Jul 1767 for stealing sugar, transported to VA Sep 1767 by the* Justitia], Runaway English Convict Servant, brisk, lively and full of spirit. From Robert Phillips of Fredericksburg, VA. (VG 28 Jan 1768).

McKinlay, William, about 23, Runaway Irish Servant. From Francis Thomas near Sugarloaf Mountain, Frederick Co, MD. (VG 13 Oct 1775).

Macoun, Thomas, no age given, impudent Irishman who can speak broad Scotch. From Robert Chesley, St Mary's Co, Potowmack River, MD. (VG 10-17 Aug 1739).

Maddin, Cornelius, no age stated but with hair "grey with age", Irish Servant. From Capt Robert Dudley of King & Queen Co, VA. (VG 2-9 Feb 1739).

Madrey, Darling, about 21, Runaway Soldier Deserter from 3rd Regiment of NC enlisted in Bute Co, NC, tall and dark. From Lieut William Linton. (VG 9 May 1777).

Madrey, William, no age given, Runaway Soldier Deserter from 3rd Regiment of NC enlisted in Bute Co, NC, short and dark. From Lieut William Linton. (VG 9 May 1777).

Magruder alias Redurgam, Nathaniel, no age given, ran away with two negro orphan boys belonging to James Benn. From Joseph Wright, Isle of Wight Co., VA. (VG 8-15 Apr 1737).

Mahany, John, about 25, Suspected Runaway Servant detained in Essex Co Jail, VA, who says he was imported in about 1771 from Cork, Ireland, in a ship commanded by John Roberts and was sold at Quantico, VA, to William Steward of Pittsylvania, VA. The owner to approach the jailer James Emerson. (VG 5 Jan 1776).

Mallert, Thomas, no age given, sent by the advertiser to command a sloop to Baltimore, MD, where he misbehaved and absconded to some part of VA; he is very dark, pox ridden and remarkably smooth spoken. From Joseph Dashiell of Somerset Co, MD. (VG 10 Nov 1774).

Malone, Patrick, about 20, Runaway Irish Indented Servant who speaks quick a good deal on the brogue. From James Franklin near Baltimore Town, MD. (VG 1 Apr 1773).

Man, Francis, no age stated, [*sentenced Apr1738 at Middlesex Sessions for stealing six handkerchiefs, transported to VA Jun 1738 by the* Forward], Englishman with yellow rotten teeth. From William Aylett of Westmoreland Co, VA. (VG 10-17 Aug 1739).

Mariner, George, about 30, Runaway born in New England, deserted the snow *Industrious Bee* at Sandy Point, VA. From Henry Pascal of the said vessel. (VG 5 Jun 1752).

Markland, John, 16-17, Runaway Apprentice Boy, knock-kneed and with thick lips, last seen aboard the snow *Lord Stanley* and is imagined to have gone to Jamaica to work in the printing business in which he was brought up. From Hugh Gaine living in New York. (VG 3 Sep 1772).

Marr, William, about 30, Runaway Irish Servant who crossed over the Potomac below Ockoquan, VA, and has been seen in MD. From Charles Chiswell of Hanover Co, VA. (VG 18-25 Feb 1737).

Marshal, Edward, no age given, below middle stature, very talkative and given to liquor, not long discharged from the cruiser *Raleigh*, Runaway Deserter Soldier of 8th Regiment. From Edward Moody, Williamsburg, VA. (VG 16 Aug 1776).

Marshall, Mary, no age stated, Runaway Irish Servant who ran with a mulatto man. From John Chiswell of Hanover Co, VA. (VG 17 Oct 1751).

Martin, Christopher, no age given, Suspected Runaway Irish Servant of genteel countenance who says he belongs to Matthias Bodeley of Cecil Co, MD. From Lewis Neill of Frederick Co Gaol, VA. (VG 17 Oct 1751).

Martin, Frank, no age stated, Runaway Freeman, tall and well made. From John Atkinson of Fredericksburg, VA. (VG 19 Mar 1772).

Martin, James, about 25, Runaway Irish Deserter, a little marked with smallpox, from the galley *Hero*. From Capt George Muter of said vessel. (VG 26 Jul 1776).

Martin, John, no age given, Runaway Welsh Servant who speaks very broken English. From James Armstrong of Augusta Co, VA. (VG 7 Nov 1754).

Martin, Oliver, 22, [*transported for life from Surrey Assizes in Lent 1773 and shipped in Jul 1773 to VA in the* Tayloe], Runaway Irish Convict Servant who ran from the *Tayloe* at Four Mile Creek, VA. He was born in Ireland, looks pert and well and is by trade a carpenter and joiner. From Sampson & George Mathews, Williamsburg, VA. (VG 11 Nov 1773).

Martin, Richard, about 22, Runaway Sailor from Capt McCarty's plantation at Pope's Creek, Westmoreland Co, VA. From Augustine Washington, Prince William Co, VA. (VG 2-9 Jun 1738).

Martin, Thomas, 26, Runaway Irishman pitted with smallpox, from the *Industrious Bee* at Sandy Point, VA. From Henry Pascal of the said vessel. (VG 5 Jun 1752).

Martin, Thomas, about 25, Runaway Deserter Soldier of 5th Battalion enlisted in Bedford. From Capt Harry Terrell, Williamsburg, VA. (VG 27 Sep 1776).

Maskall (Mascall), Thomas, about 26, [*sentenced Summer 1738 at Berkshire Assizes, reprieved for 14 years' transportation in Lent 1739*], Runaway English Servant, swarthy and talks broad. From George Turberville of Westmoreland Co, VA. (VG 13-20 Jul 1739).

Mason, John, no age given, [perhaps the one of that name sentenced at Essex Assizes and reprieved to be transported to VA for 14 years in Oct 1768 by the *Justitia*], Runaway Servant lately cut over one eye, by trade a peruke maker. From David Reynolds in Norfolk, VA. (VG 12 May 1774).

Mason, John, 22-23, Runaway Servant, barber, stoops in his walk. From Walter Lenox, Pinkney, VA. (VG 13 Jul 1775).

Matheson (Mathison), David, about 25, Runaway Scottish Indented Servant, gardener by trade. From William Brent in Stafford Co, VA. (VG 5 & 7 Jan 1775).

Matthews, Francis, 19-20, Runaway Irish Convict Servant, thin made, stooped walk, a scar over his right eye and much pitted with smallpox. From Philip Hall, near Snoden's Ironworks, Prince George Co, MD. (VG 21 Sep 1775).

Matthews, Jude, about 25, Runaway Irish Servant. From Coleman Read of Westmoreland Co, VA. (VG 10-17 Aug 1739).

Matthews, Paul, no age given, [*probably transported from Middlesex Sessions by the in Jul 1770*], Suspected Runaway Convict Servant, who says he belongs to John Struther of Culpeper Co, VA, and now in Westmoreland Co Gaol. Owner to contact gaoler James Muse. (VG 9 Mar 1775).

Mattox, Mary, no age given, wife of William Mattox (q.v.). A small slender woman pitted with smallpox. From William Tinsley near Hanover Town, VA. (VG 18 Aug 1774).

Mattox, William, no age given, Runaway Indented Servant, tall and thin, commonly has sore eyes and is much pitted with smallpox. From William Tinsley near Hanover Town, VA. (VG 18 Aug 1774).

Maund, Nicholas, about 45, [*probably to be identified with Nicholas Lloyd alias Maund sentenced to transportation at Worcester Assizes in Summer 1761*], Runaway Convict Servant, wheelwright and wagon maker by trade, born in Yorkshire who speaks the dialect very much; known worker in most parts of MD & VA. From Joseph Cross near Newgate, Loudoun Co, VA. (VG 2 Dec 1773).

May, Thomas, no age given, Runaway Regular Soldier Deserter at York, VA; he was born in King & Queen Co, VA, where he is probably now harboured. From Gregory Smith, Williamsburg, VA. (VG 22 Nov 1776).

McCann, Peter, no age given, Suspected Runaway Servant but fits the description of a servant of Robert Rutherford; he says he is a schoolmaster in King George Co. Owner to apply to Richard Baker at Isle of Wight Co Gaol, VA. (VG 19 Jul 1770).

McCartney, Nicholas, about 27, Runaway Irish Servant much pitted with smallpox, by trade a shoemaker. From Zachariah Hendrick, Cumberland Co, VA. (VG 17 Feb 1774).

McCarty, Daniel, about 19, Runaway Apprentice, stout-limbed, very apt to give fancy language when spoken to, he works at the wheelwright business. From William Cosby, Williamsburg, VA. (VG 9 Jan 1772).

McClean, Matthew, about 24, Runaway Deserter from HMS *Fowey* in Hampton Road, VA. From Policarpus Taylor, Capt of said ship. (VG 3-10 Oct 1745).

McClure, William, no age given, Runaway Soldier Deserter from 2nd Battalion for Georgia. From Joseph Pannill, Prince Edward Courthouse, VA. (VG 27 Dec 1776).

McConnelly, John, no age given, Runaway Soldier Deserter from 2nd Battalion for Georgia. From Joseph Pannill, Prince Edward Courthouse, VA. (VG 27 Dec 1776).

McCraw, Daniel, no age given, Runaway Scots-Highlander, short and speaking broken English. From Charles Dick in Fredericksburg, VA. Charles Dick in Fredericksburg, VA. VG 7-14 Aug 1746).

McCue (Mackue), John, no age given, [*sentenced at Middlesex Sessions for stealing iron gates Jan & transported Jun 1738 to VA by the* Forward], Runaway Irish Servant of middle stature, swarthy complexion, his hair is just cut off, and is a blacksmith by trade; he has on one of his arms a bleeding heart, pricked with gunpowder, and a name at length, a blacksmith by trade. From John Bushrode of Westmoreland Co, VA. (10-17 Aug 1739).

McDaniel, James, no age given, Runaway Irish Servant who has escaped from Edenton Gaol, VA. From J McDowell of said Gaol. (VG 13-20 Jun 1745).

McDaniel, Thomas, no age given, a tailor, Runaway Soldier Deserter from 8th Battalion in Williamsburg, VA. From James Higgin, Williamsburg. (VG 13 Dec 1776).

McDonald, Alexander, no age given, Runaway Scottish Highland Convict Servant who ran from the ship *Donald* at Four Mile Creek, Richmond, VA, in his own country garb. From James McDowall and Robert Burton in Richmond. (VG 15 Apr 1773).

McDonald, Dennis, no age given, Runaway Indented Servant with a remarkable scar on his left leg and another on his right instep occasioned by a scald. From George Norvell in Hanover Co, VA. (VG 16 Jun 1774).

McDonald, James (1769) – *See* Daniel, Edward.

McDonald alias McDaniel, James, 20, Runaway Irish Convict, labourer formerly in possession of John Hook, merchant in Bedford, NC, who sold him to merchants Chambers & Montgomery in Salisbury NC from whom he fled. Owner to approach Peter Pelham, Jailer of Williamsburg, VA. (VG 27 Oct 1774).

McDonald, William, no age given, Runaway Indentured Servant from North Scotland who has been about a year in the country, is marked with smallpox and has red hair; by trade a cooper. From Gardner Fleming of Williamsburg, VA. (VG 8 Oct 1767).

McDowel, Samuel, about 32, born at Newport, Glasgow, has a large black beard and talks broad Scotch; deserted from the ship *Berry*. From James Belcher at Sheppard's Warehouse, Williamsburg, VA. (VG 27 Mar 1752).

McFarlan, Frederick, about 23, Runaway Mulatto Servant who was seen boarding a ship bound to Nansemond. From John Stuart near Boyd's Hole, Stafford, VA. (VG 8 Nov 1770).

McFarlan, Robert, no age given, Runaway Scottish Servant who talks broad and whose arm has been broken. From Alexander Rose on plantation of Rev Robert Rose of Albemarle Co deceased. (VG 5 Mar 1752).

McFarling, James, no age given, Arrested Servant suspected of stealing two negroes. Owners to apply to James Atkinson & Barnabas Lorrain of Norfolk, VA. (VG 19 Nov 1772).

McGill, Andrew, no age given, Runaway Scottish Servant, a blacksmith, by trade a blacksmith. From John Shipard, Williamsburg, VA. (VG 29 Jul 1775).

McGinnis, Daniel, no age given, Suspected Runaway Irish Schoolmaster with much of the brogue who has absconded from Williamsburg, VA. From Andrew Meek of Williamsburg. (VG 4 Aug 1774).

McGuier, Thomas (1752) – *See* Guier.

McLane, James, no age stated, Runaway Convict Servant who ran from the schooner *Occoquan* lying in Yeocomico River, VA; he is well made and has a bold countenance. From John Tayloe, Williamsburg, VA. (VG 24 Dec 1772).

McLane, James, no age given, Runaway Scottish Indented Servant of the most unparalleled ingratitude who ran away last winter from a schooner in Potomac River; talks much of his feats in the last war. From Thomas Lawson, Neabsco Furnace, Prince William Co, VA. (VG 24 Jun & 8 Jul 1773).

McLean, James, about 28, Suspected Runaway Scottish Servant, stout made and has lost a finger on his right hand. From Samuel Wood at Richmond, VA. (VG 27 Oct 1774).

McLoughlin, James, no age given, Runaway Irish Servant with scars on the head who has escaped from Edenton Gaol, VA. From J McDowell of said Gaol. (VG 13-20 Jun 1745).

McMerton, Cornelius, 30-40, Runaway Irish Servant. From Richard Boatman of Lancaster Co, VA. (VG 15-22 Oct 1736).

McQueen, Daniel, transported from Surrey Assizes by the *Caesar* in 1736. Runaway English Convict born in London and bred a waterman, about 21, small and thin. From Benjamin Porter near the South West Mountains, Orange Co, VA. (VG 27 Oct-3 Nov 1738).

McQuire, Patrick, about 45, Suspected Runaway Scottish Servant, thick made and of rascally aspect, much addicted to drink, by trade a smith and farrier. From Samuel Wood at Richmond, VA. (VG 27 Oct 1774).

McWilliam, William, no age given, Runaway Scottish Highland Convict Servant who ran from the ship *Donald* at Four Mile Creek, Richmond, VA, in his own country garb. From James McDowall and Robert Burton in Richmond. (VG 15 Apr 1773).

Merryman, Thomas, no age given, Runaway Marine Deserter from the cruiser *Muskito* lying at Warwick, VA, who has an inoffensive look and is probably gone to Caroline Co, VA, where he lives. From Jacob Valentine in Richmond Town, VA. (VG 13 Sep 1776).

Messer, John, no age given, Runaway Dutch Servant with reddish hair who talks good English and went away with his wife. From James Meroney, Williamsburg, VA. (VG 13 Apr 1769).

Miers, Sarah, no age given, Runaway Dutch Servant who talks broken English, tall and round shouldered. From Patrick Creagh of Annapolis, MD. (VG 8-15 Oct 1736).

Miller, John, about 28, [an upholsterer who was convicted in Sep at Middlesex Sessions in Sep 1766 of stealing a gold-headed cane and in Jan 1767 transported to VA on the *Tryal*], Runaway English Convict Servant with a large scar on his forehead who has been in the country before, talks very much and is deceitful. From William Carr Lane near Rocky Run Chapel, Loudoun Co, VA. (VG 12 May 1768).

Mills, Robert, about 22, [*sentenced in Mar 1771 at Somerset Assizes to be transported and shipped in Jul 1771 to MD*], Runaway Irish Servant, imported as a gardener in September last by Capt Joseph Street. From Samuel Hanson, Charles Co, MD. (VG 24 Nov 1774).

Milson, Charles, no age given, Suspected Runaway Servant confined to Botetourt Co Jail, VA, who says he belongs to Robert Anner in Hannah's Town, Westmoreland Co, PA. The owner to contact Sheriff Francis Smith. (VG 23 Jun 1775).

Milven, Robert, no age given, Runaway Scottish Seaman from the *Encouragement* of London lying at West Point, VA. From Alexander Douglas of the said ship. (VG 10 Apr 1752).

Minor, Henry, about 16, Runaway Apprentice Lad, very freckled and with red hair; he was recently taken up in Caroline Co but escaped. From Richard Holt Jr in Essex Co, VA. (VG 15 Mar 1770).

Minor, John, about 26, Runaway Servant, plasterer by trade but can work as glazier and bricklayer, disfigured by smallpox. From John Lewis of Gloucester Co, VA. (**VG** 21-28 Apr 1738).

Mitchell, James (1739) - *See* Cambell.

Mobbs, Martha, about 24, [*sentenced at London Sessions in Jun 1738 for stealing clothing, transported to VA by the* Dorsetshire *in Jan 1739*]. From William Roane of Essex Co, VA. (VG 28 Sep-5 Oct 1739).

Molloy, John, no age given, Runaway Irish Sailor who deserted the ship *Fairfield* now lying at Norfolk, VA. From Capt Gawin Hamilton. (VG 3 Jan 1771).

Molloy, Patrick, about 20, Runaway Irish Servant who appears silly but is very deceitful and marked with smallpox. From David Boyd in Northumberland Co, VA. (V 29 Oct 1767).

Moncrief, Henry, about 30, Runaway Scottish Servant who speaks broad and has been used to the sea, his left arm is longer than the right. From Isaac Zane of Frederick Co, VA. (VG 12 Sep 1777).

Money alias Mooney, Nicholas, no age given, of Greenbriar, VA, Runaway Deserter Recruit raised for the Georgia Service. From Robert & George Walton at Prince Edward Courthouse. (VG 27 Sep 1776).

Monroe, John, 27, [*sentenced at Northumberland Assizes to be transported and awaiting transportation in Summer 1765*], Runaway Convict of sallow complexion, an apothecary. From Patrick Coutts on James River, Richmond, VA. (VG 16 May 1766).

Mooney, Nicholas (1776) – *See* Money.

Moore, James, no age given, Runaway Irish Servant, short and thick with a piece out of his right nostril who pretends to be a doctor; supposedly gone to NC. From John Schoolar, Caroline Co, VA. (VG 25 Jan-1 Feb 1740).

Morgan, John, 21, born in London, pitted with smallpox, Runaway Seaman who deserted the sloop of war *American Congress* in Yeocomico, Northumberland Co, VA. From John Allison, Capt of Marines of said vessel. (VG 21 Jun 1776).

Morgan, Mark, about 26, of Essex Co, VA, tall and well-set with yellow complexion who lived for some time on New River, NC, and perhaps will return there. From Thomas Thorp, Upper End, Essex Co, VA. (VG 8-15 Dec 1738).

Morgan, William, no age given, [*sentenced at London Sessions for stealing a handkerchief in Dec 1764 and transported to VA in Feb 1765 by the* Trial], Runaway English Convict Servant, pitted with smallpox. From Edward Hill of Blandford, Prince George Co, VA. (VG 23 Jul 1766)

Morris, James, no age stated, Runaway Welsh Servant, house carpenter and joiner, supposed to be heading for Carolina. From Harry Gaines from estate of William Byrd at Westover, VA. (VG 27Mar 1752).

Morris alias Morrison, William, no age given, Runaway Irish Servant who has a lame left leg and arm now committed to Augusta Co Gaol, VA. His master to apply to George Matthews, Sheriff of Augusta. (VG 31 Oct 1771).

Morrison, Clowd, no age given, Indented Scottish Servant, shoemaker, broad spoken, good scholar much pitted with smallpox, shoemaker who may make for NC. From Archibald Midlimist, James French's shop in Petersburg, VA. (VG 2 May 1777).

Morrison, William (1771) – See Morris.

Moss, John, no age given, Runaway English Servant. From William Foster in Forks of James River, Botetourt Co VA. (VG 30 Sep 1773).

Mulrain, Thomas, about 25, Servant born in St Kitts but chiefly bred in Scotland, has served 7 years with 5 more to come, formerly servant to John Combs of Shenandoah, VA. From Bartholomew Fryatt of Middle Creek, Frederick Co, VA. (VG 12 Jul 1770).

Murdy, George, about 20, Runaway Irish Servant. From George Sell in Frederick Co, VA. (VG 8 Mar 1776).

Murfy, Charles, Runaway Servant belonging to Mrs Ballendine, sawyer by trade with a crucifix burned on his arm. From LeRoy Griffin of Richmond Co, VA. (VG 13-20 May 1737).

Murphey, Francis alias Roberts, Charles, middle aged, Suspected Runaway Servant pitted with smallpox, who can give only a slender account of himself and now committed to James City Co Gaol, VA. (VG 2-9 Nov 1739).

Murphey, John, no age given, [probably the John Murphy who was sentenced in May 1771 at Middlesex Sessions for stealing a diamond ring & transported to MD in Jul 1771 by the *Scarsdale*], Runaway English Convict Servant who speaks plain and writes well. From John May, Botetourt Co, VA. (VG 17 Nov 1775).

Murphy, James (1751). See Keays .

Murphey, Patrick, no age given, Suspected Runaway Irish Servant who has not confessed any master and speaks very bad English; he is much pitted with smallpox and is believed to have come from MD. Owner to apply to Francis Triplett, gaoler of Prince William Co Gaol. (VG 27 Apr 1769).

Murray, Michael, about 21, Runaway Irish Convict. From Edward Stevenson of Little Pipe Creek, Frederick Co, MD. (VG 11 Jun 1767).

Murroe, John, no age stated, Irish Servant. From Matthew Kenner, Wicomoco River,VA. (VG 3-10 Nov 1738).

Nabb, John (1738) – *See* Coleman.

Nainby, William, no age given, Suspected Runaway English Lad committed to Amherst Gaol , VA. Owner to apply to gaoler William Pollard. (VG 21 Sep 1776).

Nash, William, no age given, Runaway English Convict by trade a bricklayer with a large black beard and flat nose, much given to drink; ran from plantation of John Willis in Brunswick Co, VA, and supposedly gone to NC. From Augustine Smith of Brunswick Co. (VG 2-9 May 1745).

Neale, Edward, no age stated, Runaway Indentured Irish Servant , barber. From John Stevenson, Baltimore Town, MD. (VG 27 Jul 1769).

Neal, Thomas, no age given, Runaway stocking weaver from the snow *Fortune*, Capt. William Rowntree, lately wrecked in Chesapeake Bay. From George Brown, of Kingston, VA. (VG 5 Oct 1769).

Neale, William, no age stated, Runaway Irish Convict Servant, bald on the back of his head. From William Ficklin of King George Co, VA.

Neavers, John, no age given, Runaway English Servant with big wrists and hands. From Thomas Blincoe and Hardage Lane of Loudoun Co, VA. (VG 18 Jan 1770).

Newton, George, no age given, Runaway Convict Servant born in Yorkshire and imported (*from London Quarter Sessions*) to VA in the *Justitia*, six feet tall, stout with a red beard and walks clumsily; he worked in an office near the London Custom House. From James Tutt, Duncan, Norfolk, VA. (VG 15 Jun 1775).

Newton, John, about 20, Runaway Asiatic Indian Servant who has been in VA about a year but formerly was ten years in England as servant of Sir Charles Whitworth; has a very sour look and was last seen wearing a postilion's coat; he was in the service of George Rootes of Frederick Co and Col Blackburn of Prince William Co and is a good barber and hairdresser. From William Brown of Williamsburg, VA. (VG 13 & 19 Jul 1776).

Nicholls, William, no age stated, [*sentenced to transportation at Worcestershire Assizes Lent 1771 for stealing linen at Kidderminster*], Runaway Servant, native of England, served his time with John Golat near Difficult Run, Fairfax Co, VA, then engaged as gunsmith's journeyman and left a wife in Prince George Co, MD., From Stephen West, Prince George Co. (VG 14 Nov 1776).

Nicholson, William, about 21, Runaway English Convict Servant pitted with smallpox (*transported from Southwark Sessions in Apr 1772*). From John Kidd, Commander of the *Thornton* lying at Leeds Town, VA. (VG 23 Jul 1772).

Nives, William, about 20, Runaway Servant, a low squat fellow. From William Withers, Fauquier Co, Ca. (VG 23 Apr 1772).

Noland, Thomas, 24-25, Irish Servant, freckled and red headed, good joiner who writes well. From Richard Arell of Alexandria, VA. (VG 23 May 1771).

Noonan, William, no age given, Runaway Irish Servant who walks quickly, has a scar over his eye and the brogue in his dialect. From John Baird, Appomatox, VA. (VG 23 Feb 1775).

Norris, Alexander, no age given, Runaway Scottish Servant, by trade a house carpenter seen at Aquia asking the way to Fredericksburg, VA. From Reginald Graham in Dumfries, VA. (VG 31 Mar 1775).

Norris, Thomas, no age given, Runaway Servant with a scar on his forehead who is imagined to have gone to Carolina, by trade a tailor. From Philip Grymes of Williamsburg, VA. (VG 13 Feb 1752).

Norris, William, no age given, Runaway Servant, well set with a pot belly and flat nose, (*probably transported from Norfolk Assizes in Summer 1771*). From Edward Stevenson, Little Pipe Creek, Frederick Co, MD. (VG 12 Mar 1772).

Nouchtie, James, about 22, Runaway Scottish Servant who broke open a shop window. From Andrew Cubbin of Petersburg, VA. (VG 27 Apr 1769).

Nugent, Andrew, no age given, Runaway Irish Servant with short and slovenly hair, a downy beard, round shouldered, a scar on his forehead and distinctly pitted with smallpox; a house joiner by trade who recently asked the way to Newcastle. From Stephen Johnston of Williamsburg, VA. (VG 24 Oct 1771).

O'Brian, John (1775) – *See* Brenon.

O'Brien, John, about 21, Indented Irish Servant, tailor by trade, pitted with smallpox and with a remarkably long head. From William Davis of York Town, VA. (VG 24 Jan 1777).

O'Brien, Matthew, no age given, Suspected Runaway Servant thought to be the one advertised as Matthew Tharp (q.v.). His master to claim him from Nathaniel Terry of Halifax Gaol. (VG 6 May 1773).

O'Conner, Francis, no age given, Runaway Irish Servant. From Thomas Nevett of Cambridge, Great Choptank River, MD. (VG 15-22 Oct 1736).

O'Daniel, James (1774) – *See* Colloney, Richard.

O'Neal, Timothy, 22. Runaway Irish Servant who has a small scar on an eyebrow and calls himself a barber; he was seen a little above Fredericksburg, VA. From James Kennerly near Wood's Gap, Augusta Co, VA. (VG 5 Sep 1771).

Ocinhyser, John, no age given, Runaway Dutch Servant, a baker by trade who talks broken English with a smiling countenance. From Peter Bowers in King George Co, VA. (VG 24 Feb 1775).

Ogle, Thomas, no age stated, Runaway Servant who says he is English but appears to be Irish, has a one inch scar on his face, very artful, formerly the property of Hugh Houston of Fredericksburg, VA. From Benjamin Johnston of Fredericksburg. (VG 20 Oct 1774).

Olderage, Godlip, about 28, very talkative and pretends to understand the sea, by trade a tailor. From Robert Hutchings of Petersburg, VA. (VG 22 Sep 1752).

Orange, James, Runaway Sergeant Deserter from the British Forces who went to General Washington's Camp but refused money for his expenses in so doing. From Landon Carter near Williamsburg, VA. (VG 27 Jun 1777).

Ord, Ralph (1736) – See Taylor.

Owens, Thomas, no age given, Runaway Servant believed guilty of robbing Josias Cook of Pittsylvania Co, VA. Instruction by John Wilson for him and two others to be apprehended. (VG 28 Apr 1775).

Owens, William, no age stated, Runaway Servant, a cooper. From James Campbell & Co, Norfolk, VA. (VG 15 Feb 1770).

Owl, John alias Layne, William, about 35, Runaway Servant, large and fat with a red beard and slight squint who has a scarified wrist from wearing fetters. From James Findly of Albemarle Co, VA. (VG 11-18 Apr 1745).

Oxen, William alias Pursell, Anthony, no age given. Suspected Runaway Irish Servant in Williamsburg Public Gaol, VA, who says he belongs to Robert Walker of Essex Co, VA. His master may have him on payment of charges to William Wyatt of the said gaol. (VG 21-28 Aug 1746).

Palmer, Charles, no age given, Runaway Apprentice enlisted by Thomas Armistead during advertiser's absence. From Nathaniel Fox, King William Co, VA. (VG 14 Feb 1777).

Parfett (Perfect), Christopher, about 19, [sentenced at Surrey Assizes and transported to VA in Apr 1739 by the *Forward*], Runaway English Convict. From George Turberville of Westmoreland Co, VA. (VG 13-20 Jun 1739).

Page, Thomas, no age given, [of St. Leonard Shoreditch, Mddx, sentenced at Middlesex Sessions in Apr 1744 for stealing gold rings and transported to VA by *Justitia* in May 1744], barber and wigmaker who lived most of his time in London, much given to drink; his mother Martha Page found not guilty of receiving]). From William Taite of Williamsburg, VA. (VG 14-21 Nov 1745).

Park, James, no age given, Runaway Deserter from the ship *Hanbury* lying in Mattapony River, of which he was mate. From James Esten of the said ship. (VG 30 Apr 1767). Declaration by James Park that the accusation is false and he would not have left the ship but for the ill treatment he received from the boatswain. (VG 14 May 1767).

Park, Stephen, about 45, English born house carpenter & joiner, remarkable for hard drinking and swearing. From Thomas Williamson of Southampton Co, VA. (VG 18 Apr 1751).

Parker, James, no age given, Runaway Deserter Soldier from 2nd Battalion for Georgia. From Joseph Pannill, Prince Edward Courthouse, VA. (VG 27 Dec 1776).

Parker, Richard, Runaway Irish Soldier Deserter, 35-40, a slovenly fellow much addicted to liquor. From Lieut John R Davies, Williamsburg, VA. (VG 24 Jan 1777).

Parker, Thomas, no age stated, native of Philadelphia. From Matthew Kenner, Wiccomoco River, VA. (VG 3-10 Nov 1738).

Parker, William, 21, Indented English Servant, by trade a blacksmith but since being in VA a waiting man, of quick speech. From Archibald McKendrick, Richmond, VA. (VG 3 Mar 1775).

Parks, James, no age given, Runaway Deserter Seaman of sloop of war *Scorpion*. From Wright Westcott, Yeocomico, VA. (VG 23 Aug 1776).

Parmer, John, 13-14, apprentice tailor. From Edward Maxey near Flat Rock, Cumberland Co, VA. (VG 16 Feb 1769).

Parrot, Benjamin, 32, Runaway Indented Servant, born in London, house carpenter by trade who came to VA by the ship *Elizabeth* in April 1774. From Joshua Poythress, Flower de Hundred, Prince George Co. (VG 16 Jun 1774).

Partin, William, 35, Virginian Deserter. From Capt Alexander Finnie. Reward offered by Thomas Cocks, Williamsburg, VA. (VG 28 Feb 1755).

Past, John, no age stated, Runaway English Servant who could be taken for a mulatto. From Andrew Johnson near Augusta Co Courthouse, VA. (VG 18 Jul 1751).

Patterson, George, no age given, Runaway Deserter Seaman, boatswain of sloop of war *Scorpion* who has a snub nose. From Wright Westcott, Yeocomico, VA. (VG 23 Aug 1776).

Paterson, James, about 25, [sentenced at Middlesex Sessions in Dec 1762 for stealing lump sugar and transported in Mar 1763 by the *Neptune*; his wife Ann Paterson found not guilty], Runaway Servant born in Scotland, much pox-ridden, by trade a shoemaker. From William Trebell of Williamsburg. (VG4 Nov 1763).

Patterson (Patteson), James, no age stated, Runaway Servant Lad imported on the *Betsy*, Capt Ramsay, who ran away in Apr 1772 from Alexander Gordon, near the Long Bridge, Charles City Co, VA., changed his name and got aboard the said ship to escape the country (VG 23 Apr 1772); he ran again from the same master in 1773. (VG 7 Jan 1773).

Patterson, James, 20, decoyed to Louisa or Albemarle Co by his father, Runaway Soldier Deserter from 6th Virginia Regiment. From Capt Thomas Massie of said Regiment. (VG 11 Jul 1777).

Payne, Joseph, about 25, Runaway Deserter Soldier enlisted in Bedford, from 5th Battalion, Williamsburg, VA. From Gross Scruggs, Williamsburg. (VG 27 Sep 1776).

Pearle, Richard, 32, born in VA, stout, artful and ill-looking, Runaway Seaman who deserted the sloop of war *American Congress* in Yeocomico, Northumberland Co, VA. From John Allison, Capt of Marines of said vessel. (VG 21 Jun 1776).

Peart, George, about 22, Runaway English Indented Servant born in Co Durham, pitted with smallpox who pretends to be a shoemaker. From Andrew Leitch living in Dumfries, VA. (VG 4 May 1775).

Pebworth, Robert, about 23, Servant, weaver, "has wrote himself a pass." From Francis Searson, of Prince William Co, VA. (VG 3-10 Aug 1739).

Peed, Thomas, no age given, Runaway Soldier Deserter from Capt Charles Tomkies' Co of 7th Regiment and probably now in Gloucester Co, VA, where it was raised. From Reuben Lipscomb, Williamsburg, VA. (VG 24 Jan 1777).

Pellawn, James, about 16, Runaway Irish Servant Boy, pale-faced from ague and fever, supposed to have gone towards Norfolk, VA. From Edward Stabler, Williamsburg, VA. (VG 3 Jan 1771).

Penn, Solomon, no age given, Runaway Irish Servant from the Greenvale at Ruffin's Ferry, Pamunky River, weakly made with a puny complexion. From Thomas Ritchie of the said ship. (VG 19 Apr 1770).

Pentecost, James, no age given, [sentenced at London Sessions for forgery Oct, transported in Dec 1767 to VA by the *Neptune* in Dec 1767 and landed in Jan 1768], Convict Servant, pitted with smallpox and carrying £20 imported on said ship. From Richard Johnston of Culpeper Courthouse, VA. (VG 21 Sep 1769).

Perry, Thomas, about 27, [perhaps the convict transported from the Yorkshire Assizes in Lent 1737],Welsh Runaway Servant, left leg shorter than the right and a scar on his forehead who says he is a shoemaker, wigmaker and glazier. Committed to Public Prison in Williamsburg, VA. (VG 1-18 Jun 1739).

Peters, Abraham, about 28, [sentenced to death at London Sessions for shoplifting, reprieved to be transported for 14 years in Apr 1770 and transported in the same month to MD by the *Thornton*], Runaway English Servant who has a perished and lame left hand who says he is a Jew and speaks good Dutch. From Buckler Bond living near Bush River, Harford Co, MD. (VG 21 Apr 1775).

Peters, John, more than 30, [sentenced at Kent Assizes and transported to VA in May 1737 by the *Forward*], Runaway Convict Servant speaks broad and is about six foot tall and round-shouldered. From George Sinclaire of Stafford Co, VA. (VG 28 Oct – 4 Nov 1737).

Petheram. James Batier, about 26, Runaway English Servant and pretended coachman who has been in the country a year. From Lemuel Riddick of Suffolk Town, VA. (VG 6 Oct 1752).

Pettit, Thomas, no age given, Deserter from Capt John Blair's Co of 9th Virginia Regiment when under marching orders. From Lieut Thomas Overton, Williamsburg, VA. (VG 11 Jul 1777).

Phillips, John, young man, Runaway Deserter from 6th Regiment of Continental Regulars, forward and talkative. From Nicholas Hobson of said Regiment. (VG 26 Jul 1776).

Philips, Mary (1773) – See Davis.

Phillips, Richard, no age given, of Louisa Co, VA, Runaway Soldier Deserter from 15th Continental Battalion. From Capt William Grimes, Williamsburg, VA. (VG 28 Mar 1777).

Philips alias Hamilton, Thomas, about 25, [probably the Thomas Phillips convicted for breaking and entering at Middlesex Sessions in Dec 1771 & transported in the same month to VA in the *Justitia*], Convict Runaway Servant who says he was born in Herefordshire, very talkative and addicted to swearing and drinking; probably has a 19 years old woman with him. From William Thompson, tailor near Boyd's Hole, Stafford Co, VA. (VG 11 Mar 1773).

Pickford, Charles, about 25, Runaway English Servant, bricklayer by trade with bald head. From Hon John Carter of Shirley, Charles Co, VA. (VG23030 Nov 1739).

Pierce, Isabella, alias Castillo, Bridget, no age given. From Thomas Lewis, Fairfax Co, VA. (VG 2-9 May 1745).

Pierse (Pearce), William, about 25, [sentenced at London Sessions in Dec 1774 for stealing 70 lbs of sugar and transported in the same month to VA], Runaway English Convict Servant just imported in the *Justitia* lying at Leedstown, stout with red hair. From Andrew Leitch living in Dumfries, VA. (VG 22 Apr, 29 Apr & 4 May 1775).

Pinkard, Jonathan, about 23, Runaway English Indented Servant, talkative, ill limbed, knock-kneed and a little pock-marked, by trade a watchmaker. From Samuel Jeffries in Second Street, Philadelphia. (VG 29 Apr 1773).

Pitt, Gorge, no age given, [shoemaker journeyman sentenced at London Sessions for stealing shoes from a shop & transported to VA Sep 1766 by the *Justitia*], Convict Servant having served in 112th Regiment of Foot, pitted with smallpox and shot through the foot, good shoemaker. From Samuel Hipkins of Totuskey Bridge, Richmond Co, VA. (VG 25 Aug 1768).

Pobgee (Popjee), William, no age given, [sentenced at Surrey Assizes Summer 1772 & transported to VA in Jan 1773 by the *Justitia*], Runaway English Convict), slender and pock-pitted, by trade a hatter. From Sampson & George Matthews in Staunton, VA. (VG 6 May 1773).

Pollard, John, about 25, [sentenced at Middlesex Quarter Sessions in 1771 & transported to MD in Jly 1771 by the *Scarsdale*], Runaway Servant, well-set with a scar on his chest caused by a scald. From Edward Stevenson, Little Pipe Creek, Frederick Co, MD. (VG 12 Mar 1772).

Pollard, Jonathan, no age given, [sentenced at Lancashire Assizes in Summer 1764 for highway robbery & reprieved for transportation in Lent 1765], Runaway Convict Servant who has committed several robberies lately, pitted with smallpox about the nose, quarrelsome when drunk but otherwise affable and handy; a weaver by trade but calls himself a collier and pretends to be knowing about mines. From Gerard Ellyson of Chesterfield Co, VA. (VG 19 Feb 1767).

Poole. George, about 26, [sentenced at London Sessions in Jun 1769 for stealing a silk handkerchief & transported to MD in Aug 1769 by the *Douglas*], Runaway Apprentice Boy who has served two years in the tailor's business. From John Woodside of Norfolk, VA. (VG 8 Aug 1771).

Poore, James, about 18, Runaway Deserter, piper from 6th Virginia Regiment at Hanover Courthouse. From Samuel Hopkins of 6th Regt. at Deep Spring near Williamsburg, VA. (VG 16 Aug 1776).

Pottle, William, about 30, [sentenced at Berkshire Assizes Lent 1737 for stealing a mare at Bracknell & reprieved for 14 years' transportation Summer 1737], Runaway English Servant pretending to be a husbandman. From Thomas Turner, King George Co, VA. (VG 21-28 Jul 1738).

Povall, Peter of Oswestry, Shropshire, England, a joiner who sailed from Liverpool on the *Hope*, Capt Fryer in 1759 and left her in Philadelphia; a tall man with a large mole on his throat and had lost the use of his toes. Reward offered by the printer for information whether he is alive or dead. (VG 18 Jan 1770).

Powell, David, alias Evans, Francis, about 40, brickmaker by trade. Runaway from Joseph Standford of Courthouse, Westmoreland C, VA. (VG 16-23 Feb 1739).

Powell, Matthew, no age given, born near Bristol, England, Runaway Servant who straddles much in his walk caused by the pox. From Joseph Simpson of Richmond Co, VA. (VG 6 Oct 1752).

Powel, Thomas, no age given, ran away with Henry Watkins (q.v.) having stolen a horse. Reward offered by William Hobday of York Co, VA. (VG 12-19 May 1738).

Powell, William, 40 or more, Runaway Convict Servant "born in some of the island counties in England," who speaks very plain English and writes a pretty good hand. From Richard Graham of Dumfries, VA. (VG 26 Oct 1769).

Powis, Samuel, about 40, [sentenced to transportation Lent 1773 at Worcestershire Assizes for stealing a plowshare and landed in June 1773 in Baltimore, MD], Runaway Servant born in West of England who speaks broad, a small man, tailor and staymaker. From Abraham Jarrett, Baltimore, MD. (VG 4 1774).

Pratt, Thomas, 36, [sentenced at London Sessions in Oct 1772 for stealing a silver tankard & transported to VA in Jan 1773 by the *Justitia*], Runaway English Convict Servant], by trade a millwright and pump-maker . From Sampson & George Matthews in Staunton, VA. (VG 6 May 1773).

Preston, Paul, 30, [who claimed to have a wife and children in Carolina, sentenced at Middlesex Sessions in July 1773 for stealing indigo from a ship & transported in the same month to VA by the *Tayloe*], Runaway Pennsylvanian Convict Servant who escaped from the *Tayloe* on her arrival in VA. From Sampson & George Mathews, Williamsburg, VA. (VG 11 Nov 1773).

Price, John, about 18, Suspected Runaway Servant in York Gaol, VA. Owner to apply to Sheriff Robert Sheild Jr at said gaol. (VG 27 Mar 1752).

Price, Samuel, about 35, Runaway who helped steal a schooner at Sappelo Island, Georgia, the property of Patrick Mackay; the pirate is short and slim and was lately master of a schooner in Georgia. From the said Mackay. (VG 13 Jan 1776).

Proby, Thomas, no age given, [sentenced at Middlesex Sessions in July 1739 for stealing clothing & transported in Oct 1739 to VA by the ship *Duke of Cumberland*], Runaway English Convict, by trade a plasterer, pale and pox-marked face, last seen in Norfolk, VA, and believed to be concealed with a lame shoemaker and a woman of evil fame. From Richard Taliaferro, Caroline Co, VA. (VG 16-23 May 1745).

Pruce, Thomas, no age given, English Convict Servant Runaway. From Daniel & Menoah Singleton, Orange Co, VA. (VG Supp 22 Jul 1773).

Pryor, Zachariah, no age given, Runaway Soldier Deserter from Capt Charles Tomkies' Co of 7th Regiment and probably now in Gloucester Co, VA, where it was raised. From Reuben Lipscomb, Williamsburg, VA. (VG 24 Jan 1777).

Pursell, Anthony (1746) – See Oxen, William.

Puryer, Obadjah, no age given, Runaway Servant, a journeyman chairmaker. From Elkanah Deane, Palace Street, Williamsburg, Va.

Puttrell (Putterill), Thomas, no age given, Runaway Indented Servant, a Lincolnshire man, by trade a butcher but understands gardening and farming and says he knows the business of bricklaying and plastering; he can also read and write as well as keep accounts. He ran away three times after living with Isaac Parker near Richmond Town and was taken up in Bedford Co. He was imported in 1773 on the *Liberty*, Capt Rayson. From Richard Lee of Westmoreland Co VA. (VG 8 & 22 Jul 1773) & from Thomas Attwell, Westmoreland Co, VA. (VG 12 May 1774).

Quinn, John (1773) – See Donowho.

Quir, Jeremiah, no age given, Suspected Runaway Servant who says he belongs to Col John Syme at York, VA. Owner to apply to Samuel Portlock, Gaoler of Norfolk Co, VA. (VG 24 Mar 1774).

Quirk, William, no age given, leather dresser by trade and pretended soldier with an Irish pallaver who claims he was in the late expedition to Cuba. From Robert Simpson of Williamsburg, VA. (VG 13-20 Jun 1745).

Ragan, Brice, 20, (brother of Philip (q.v.), Runaway Private Soldier Deserter from 2nd Virginia Regiment in NJ who looks agreeable. From Col Alexander Spotswood of said Regiment. (VG 5 Sep 1777).

Ragan, Philip, 22, (brother of Brice (q.v.), Runaway Corporal Deserter from 2nd Virginia Regiment in NJ who speaks fierce. From Col Alexander Spotswood of said Regiment. (VG 5 Sep 1777).

Ragland, Edmund, 17, Runaway Apprentice Boy from the plantation of John Parke Custis in King & Queen Co., VA. From George Clopton Jr. (VG 4 Aug 1775).

Railey, Daniel, about 30, Suspected Runaway Irish Servant who says he was landed in SC from a ship commanded by Capt Wilson for which he had paid his passage. Owner to contact William Bell, gaoler of Orange Co Gaol, VA. (VG 13 May 1773).

Rainbird, Joseph, no age given, (almost certainly the "Jessath Rainbord" as listed in the *Virginia Gazette*), [sentenced at Kent Assizes and transported in May 1751 to VA by the *Tryal*], Runaway English Servant, cabinet maker and joiner by trade, a smooth insinuating fellow. From Richard Lee of the Naval Office in Charles Co, MD. (VG 24 Oct 1751).

Ramshaw (Ramshire), Mary, middle-aged, [sentenced at Middlesex Sessions in June 1733 for stealing a silver-tipped mug, transported to VA by the *Caesar* and landed there in July 1734], she has several scars on her face and ran away with Brian Cagan (q.v.). Reward offered by Richard Barnes of Richmond Co, VA. (VG 2-9 Jun 1738).

Randall, Samuel, about 28, Runaway English Convict Servant with a smooth complexion, a simple innocent look and inclined to be fat, by trade a bricklayer. From John Hazlegrove in Fredericksburg, VA. (VG 2 Dec 1773).

Randolph, David, Runaway Servant who worked his time in Philadelphia and with James Hunter who may carry the boy to MD or PA and sell him. From John Brockenbrough of Hobbs' Hole, Williamsburg, VA. (VG 15 Jun 1769).

Ransom, Thomas, no age given, Runaway Soldier Deserter from Capt Charles Tomkies' Co of 7th Regiment and probably now in Gloucester Co, VA, where it was raised. From Reuben Lipscomb, Williamsburg, VA. (VG 24 Jan 1777).

Ratchford, Thomas, no age given, Runaway drawer from the snow *Fortune*, Capt. William Rowntree, lately wrecked in Chesapeake Bay. From George Brown, of Kingston, VA. (VG 5 Oct 1769).

Rawlings, William, no age given, Suspected Runaway Servant who says he is the property of Francis Smith of Chesterfield, VA, now committed to Prince William Co Gaol. Owner to contact gaoler John Blanchard. (VG 14 Oct 1773).

Ray, John, no age given, Runaway Soldier Deserter from 2nd Battalion for Georgia. From Joseph Pannill, Prince Edward Courthouse, VA. (VG 27 Dec 1776).

Rector, Christopher, aged 31, sailmaker from HMS *Triton* who ran away from duty. From Matthew Whitwell of the said ship. (VG 13 Oct 1752).

Redmond (Redman), Francis, no age given, [said to have been born and bred in Ireland, sentenced at Middlesex Sessions in Feb 1766 for robbery with violence but reprieved and transported to VA in Sep 1766 by the *Justitia*], Runaway Irish Convict Servant who has a broken cheek bone leaving a large dent in his face. From Samuel Thornbery, John Shippey and William Beavars of Loudoun Co, VA. (VG 7 Sep 1769).

Redurgam, Nathaniel (1737) – *See* Magruder.

Redman, Francis (1769) – *See* Redmond.

Reed, Henry, about 22, professed coachmaker, seen in Berkeley Co, VA. From Isaac Simmons of Herring Bay, Anne Arundel, MD.(VG 18 Aug 1774).

Read, Robert, about 40, [*sentenced at Middlesex Quarter Sessions in May and transported to VA in Sep 1766 by the* Justitia], has a pleasant countenance. From Robert Gilkison & David Hogshead near Jennings' Gap, Williamsburg, VA. (VG 27 Oct 1768).

Read, William, Indented Servant, no age given, speaks broad West Country dialect, a farmer who understands making and laying bricks. From John West, West Point, King William Co, Ca. (VG 7 Feb 1771).

Reese, David, no age given, a short slender man with a great impediment in speech Runaway Deserter Seaman of sloop of war *Scorpion*. From Wright Westcott, Yeocomico, VA. (VG 23 Aug 1776).

Reeves, James, no age given, Runaway English Servant with a scar above his eyes, born in London, a bricklayer by trade who will probably attempt to pass for a freeman. From Hugh Hicklen living in the Cow Pasture, Augusta Co, VA. (VG 7 Jun 1776).

Rennolds (Reynolds), Thomas, about 20, [sentenced at Middlesex Sessions in October 1733 for stealing a wig, transported to VA by the Caesar and landed in July 1734].Runaway Convict Servant, shoemaker of small stature. From Anne Smith of Middlesex Co, VA. (VG 17-24 Sep 1736).

Revers See Rivers.

Rice, Mary, no age given, [sentenced at Devonshire Assizes in 1751], Runaway Servant much addicted to getting drunk and to going off as his wife with a sailor. From Edward Baker of Gloucester Town, VA. (VG 10 Nov 1752).

Richardson, Alexander, about 21, [sentenced at London Sessions to transportation and shipped to MD in July 1770 by the Scarsdale], Runaway Negro Convict Servant much pox pitted and belonging to Thomas Hodge, commander of sloop Betsy in Corotoman River, Lancaster Co, VA. From said Thomas Hodge at Leeds Town, VA. (VG 7 Mar 1771)

Richardson, Charles, no age given, [sentenced at Middlesex Quarter Sessions in Sep 1767 to be transported and landed in Baltimore in Dec 1767], White Servant pitted with smallpox. From George Murrill, Albemarle Co, VA. (VG 19 Apr 1770).

Richardson, John, about 28, [sentenced at Staffordshire Assizes Lent 1772 for stealing at Shenstone, landed in Baltimore, MD, in July 1772], Convict Servant Runaway, carpenter and joiner, speaks pretty quick, supposedly gone to NC. From Sampson & George Matthews, Richmond, VA. (VG 12 Aug 1773).

Richardson, Mary, about 26, Servant committed to Prince William Co Gaol. From Gaoler John Blanchard. (VG 14 Oct 1773).

Richardson, Thomas, about 20, apprentice lad, joiner and turner, Virginia-born, talks very fast, supposed to have gone for Shenandoah, VA. From John Ball, New Kent Co, VA. (VG 24 Oct 1751).

Riddle, William, about 18, Runaway Scottish Indentured Servant born in Aberdeen who will probably make for Carolina. From William Austin of Bedford, VA. (VG 14 Sep 1769).

Rider, Edward, no age stated, Runaway English Servant lately belonging to Col Nathaniel Harrison of Brandon, much addicted to lying and a pretended Roman Catholic supposed to have gone North from New Kent Co, VA; gardener by trade. From John Hood of Prince George Co, VA. (VG 28 Mar 1751).

Ridgeway, Peter, no age given, Servant from Cheshire who speaks the country dialect, carter, plowman and husbandman. From John Tayloe, Richmond Co, VA. (VG 2-9 Jun 1738).

Riggen, Moses, 24, Virginian Deserter from Capt Carter Harrison's Co at Petersburg, VA, about 6 ft 3 ins tall, speaks slow and stoops much. (VG 24 Oct 1755).

Riley, Edward, no age given, Runaway Irish Deserter from Company of Marines at Hobb's Hole, VA, with a high fourth toe on his right foot, last seen in Fredericksburgh where he went to see a Mr Ball with whom he served his time. From Alexander Dick of said Marines Co. (VG 30 Aug 1776).

Riley, John, about 19, Indented Irish Servant, 6 feet 1 inch tall, lately seen in Prince Edward Co, VA. From Thomas Parrot, Mecklenburg, NC. (VG 1 Apr 1773).

Riley, Patrick, middle-aged, Runaway Irish Servant, a young man recently arrived in the country. From Charles Hammond Jr. & Ephraim Howard, son of Henry. (VG 26 Jul 1770).

Rivers (Revers), Robert, no age given, [sentenced at Middlesex Sessions in Oct 1773 for stealing sheep, reprieved in Dec 1773 and transported to VA in Jan 1774 by the *Justitia*], Runaway Convict Servant, by trade a shoemaker. From James Holloway at Aquia, Stafford Co, VA. (VG 28 Jul 1774).

Roach, Tynie, about 20, Runaway Convict Servant somewhat pitted with smallpox, having a smooth insinuating tongue, who has been a sailor since coming into the country four years ago and ran lately from Col Tayloe's sloop in Rappahannock. From Thomas Lawson, Neabsco Furnace, VA. (VG 24 Jun & 8 Jul 1773).

Roark, Eleanor, about 30, Runaway Servant. From William Kelly of Orange Co, VA. (VG 17-24 Apr 1746).

Robb, James, no age given, Runaway Sailor born in the North of England, deserted from the ship *Elizabeth* lying at Alexandria, VA, Capt Frederick Baker. From Robert Adam & Co, Williamsburg, VA. (VG 24 Feb 1775).

Robb, Peter, turned 30,[sentenced at Surrey Assizes of Summer 1772, reprieved and transported to VA in Jan 1773 by the *Justitia*], Runaway Scottish Convict Servant who has a sharp and artful countenance and is straight and well-made except for rather small legs; he speaks very slow and smooth and has the appearance of a sailor, by trade a baker. From McCall & Shedden's Mill near Hobb's Hole, VA. (VG 26 Aug 1773).

Roberts, Charles (1739) – *See* Murphey, Francis.

Roberts, Isaac, no age given, [sentenced in Lent 1771 at Berkshire Assizes to be transported for stealing a shilling at Newbury], Runaway Convict who speaks the Yorkshire dialect, a clumsy fellow with short black hair who pretends to be a soap maker and tallow chandler. From John Reed, Baltimore, MD. (VG 6 Feb 1772).

Roberts, Richard, 17-18, [sentenced at Middlesex Sessions in Sep 1772 for stealing silver buckles and transported to VA in Jan 1773 by the Justitia], Runaway English Convict Servant. From Benjamin Colvard and George Divers in Albemarle, Va.

Roberts, William, 44-45, Runaway English Convict Servant who has a scar on his left wrist, by trade a blacksmith. From Job Garretson near Baltimore, MD. (VG 1 Aug 1771).

Robinson, James, about 20, of Louisa Co, VA, has slightly stooped shoulders, Runaway Marine Deserter from the galley *Hero* lying at Hampton, VA. (VG 30 Aug 1776).

Robinson (Robison), John, about 28, [*probably transported from London Sessions to VA in 1765 by the Tryal*], Runaway Convict Servant, a hard looking seaman. From Andrew McClure near the Stone meeting house in Augusta, VA. (VG 23 Jun 1768).

Robinson, John, no age given, (?the same man as above), Runaway Indentured Servant pitted with smallpox who was brought up to the sea and whose name and year are marked with Indian ink on his wrist; probably intends for Baltimore, MD. From John G Frazer of West Point, King William Co, VA. (VG 4 Dec 1769).

Robinson, John, no age given, Runaway Servant of Capt John Darling of the *King of Prussia* lying at Baltimore, MD. The owner to apply to John Nevill of Frederick Co Gaol. (VG 5 Sep 1771).

Robinson, John, no age given, (brother of Thomas (q.v.). Runaway Deserter Soldier of 5th Battalion at College Camp, Williamsburg, the whites of his eyes are tinctured with jaundice, when drunk is insolent and quarrelsome; he comes from Henrico Co. From John Pleasants, Williamsburg. (VG 20 Sep 1776).

Robinson, Robert, about 28, Runaway Scottish Servant who was born in the south of that country, worked long in Edinburgh and Kelso upon Tweed and built a church at Inverness; he was purchased from on board the *Friendship*, Capt Park, from Glasgow; he speaks broad and writes well, a valuable joiner and carpenter. From Mungo Harvey in Lancaster Co, VA. (VG 23 Jun 1775).

Robinson, Thomas, about 31. Runaway Servant in Frederick Co Gaol, VA, claims he was born in Prince George Co, MD, was in England for 15 years and came from Liverpool in 1763 to land at Silvay's Landing, Patuxent, MD. From Thomas Campbell, Gaoler in Winchester, MD. (VG 30 Oct 1766).

Robinson, Thomas, no age given, (brother of John (q.v.). Runaway Deserter Soldier of 5th Battalion at College Camp, Williamsburg, who comes from Henrico Co and is somewhat deaf. From John Pleasants, Williamsburg. (VG 20 Sep 1776).

Rogers, Hugh, about 21, Runaway Indented Servant, very fond of liquor, talkative when drunk but peaceable and of few words when sober, by trade a carpenter and joiner able to use the whip saw; he came to Alexandria, VA, a year ago with Capt Coldclough from Dublin. From Thomas Rigden in George Town, VA. (VG 7 & 21 Oct 1773).

Rogers, Thomas, no age given, of Charlotte Co, VA, Runaway Deserter Recruit raised for the Georgia Service. From Robert & George Walton at Prince Edward Courthouse. (VG 27 Sep 1776).

Rolley, James, 24-25, Runaway Indented Irish Servant much pitted with smallpox with a lively brisk hand for business. From James Wood in Northampton Co, NC. (VG 23 Sep 1773).

Rollings, Philip, no age given, slender, of sallow complexion, Runaway Sailor who deserted the ship *Hoyne* at Gosport, VA. From Inglis & Long, Williamsburg, VA. (VG 31 Jan 1771).

Rollings, William, about 21, Runaway English Servant lately arrived from London, much pitted with smallpox. From Francis Smith Jr near Rocky Ridge in Chesterfield, VA. (VG 9 Sep 1773).

Ross, James, about 18, Runaway Highland Indented Scottish Servant with freckled face and red hair hanging about his shoulders; he escaped in the sloop *Lark*, Capt John Lindsay, and landed at Hardy's Ferry. From the said John Lindsay. (VG 30 Sep 1773).

Ross, John, about 16, Runaway Scots-Highland Boy who speaks broken English. From John Mitchell of Fredericksburg, VA. (VG 7-14 Aug 1746).

Row, William, 18-19, [*sentenced at London Sessions in Sep 1772 for stealing money from his master & transported to VA in Jan 1773 by the* Justitia], Runaway English Convict Servant, an artful fellow who writes a good hand and may forge a pass. From Archer Matthews living on the levels of Greenbriar, VA. (VG 16 Aug 1776).

Rowden, Abraham, about 20, full 6 feet tall, Runaway Deserter Soldier of 5th Battalion enlisted in Halifax by Capt Cox. From Capt Harry Terrell, Williamsburg, VA. (VG 27 Sep 1776).

Royston, John, 19, son of Richard Wiatt Royston of Gloucester Co, VA, Runaway Apprentice Lad with a frowning down look who may pretend to know the business of chair-making and blacksmith; he may be in Bedford or Prince William Counties. From Samuel Daniel of Middlesex Co. (VG 8 Mar 1770).

Roze, O'Brian, no age given, Suspected Runaway Servant who says he formerly belonged to Mr Birmingham but lately to John Harris of Culpeper Co, VA. He is short and thick with a sore left leg and confined to Essex Gaol. The owner to apply to the gaoler James Emerson. (VG 6 Apr 1775).

Ruark, Daniel, 22, Indented Irish Servant, tailor with many red bumps in his face, formerly belonging to Col John Smith of Richmond Co, VA. From Richard Cadden near Yeocomico church, Westmoreland Co, VA. (VG 23 Aug 1770).

Ruff, Thomas, no age given, Runaway carpenter from the snow *Fortune*, Capt. William Rowntree, lately wrecked in Chesapeake Bay. From George Brown, of Kingston, VA. (VG 5 Oct 1769).

Russell, James, no age given, Runaway Indented Servant who left in Carrituck Co, NC, and now probably lurks in Princess Ann Co. From George Woolsey of Norfolk, VA. (VG 8 Feb 1770).

Russell, Katherine, about 18, Runaway Irish Servant of red complexion. From John Smith Jr near the Courthouse, Orange Co, VA. (VG 24-31 Oct 1745).

Ryan, James, no age given, Runaway Convict Servant with a pretty large nose and smooth speech, by trade a cabinet maker. From Stephen Mitchell, York Town, VA. (VG 3 Jun 1773).

Ryan, James, 25, Runaway Irish Convict who has a long visage and full beard, formerly in possession of John Hook, merchant in Bedford NC who sold him to merchants Chambers & Montgomery in Salisbury NC from whom he fled. Owner to approach Peter Pelham, Jailer of Williamsburg, VA. (VG 27 Oct 1774).

Ryan, Thomas, Irish Convict Servant, no age given, unable to speak English. From John Fitzgerald, King William Co, VA. (VG, 18 Jun 1752).

Ryan, William, about 23, pox-ridden Irish Convict Servant who lived some time with Robert Lynn and Richard Gamble, wigmakers in Williamsburg, VA. From W Battersby of Cumberland Co, VA. (VG 10 Nov 1752).

Rylot, Edward, about 27, Runaway Servant with very bad sore shins and an ankle out of place. From Edward Stevenson, Little Pipe Creek, Frederick Co, MD. (VG 12 Mar 1772).

Sadler, Richard, no age given, Runaway Convict Servant who came in with Capt Payne two years ago and was employed to drive a cart; a very great rogue with a sly look. From John Champe of King George Co, VA. (VG 11 Apr 1755).

Salkrig, James, about 36, Runaway Scottish Servant, tailor by trade. From John Halpin, staymaker in Williamsburg, VA. (VG 23-30 Mar 1739).

Sampson, Joseph, no age given, Runaway Soldier Deserter from 2nd Battalion for Georgia. From Joseph Pannill, Prince Edward Courthouse, VA. (VG 27 Dec 1776).

Sands, Thomas, 26, Runaway Servant. From Richard Snowden, Patuxent Iron Works, MD. (VG 15-22 Jun 1739).

Saunders, John, about 18, smooth-faced, Runaway Irish Soldier Deserter from 2nd Virginia Regiment in NJ. From Col Alexander Spotswood of said Regiment. (VG 5 Sep 1777).

Saunders, Samuel, 22, Deserter from Camp at Maidstone, VA, born in MD. From Commanding Officer, Winchester, VA. (VG 27 Aug 1756).

Saunders, Samuel, 41, Runaway Indented Welsh Servant with a surly look. From Anthony Geoghegan living in Richmond Town, VA. (VG 2 Mar 1775).

Saunders, William, no age given, Runaway farmer from the snow *Fortune*, Capt. William Rowntree, lately wrecked in Chesapeake Bay. From George Brown, of Kingston, VA. (VG 5 Oct 1769).

Savage, Matthew, about 45, Indented Irish Servant, Virginia-born with relations living near Williamsburg. He indented himself in Ireland and came over with many Irish servants to Baltimore. From William Deakins Jr, George Town, Frederick Co, MD. (VG 10 Dec 1772).

Savage, Richard, no age given, Runaway Servant, tailor by trade. From Reginald Orton, York Town, VA. (VG 4-11 Mar 1737).

Savage, Simon, no age given, Runaway Soldier Deserter from 2nd Battalion for Georgia. From Joseph Pannill, Prince Edward Courthouse, VA. (VG 27 Dec 1776).

Sawyer, Charles, about 20, [*sentenced at Middlesex Quarter Sessions in Jan 1771 to be transported and shipped to MD in Apr 1771 by the* Thornton]. Runaway English Convict Servant, a Londoner and bricklayer who has lately been whipped for running away as the marks can still be seen. From Thomas Price and Thomas Michum in Annapolis, MD. (VG 2 Jun 1774).

Sayers, Robert, about 26, Runaway Servant who speaks good English, from Nathaniel Chapman, Accokeek Ironworks, Stafford Co, VA. (VG 3 Nov 1752).

Scarborough, James, 25, [*sentenced to transportation at Middlesex Sessions in Sep 1773 and taken to VA in Jan 1774 by the* Justitia], Runaway English Convict Servant who comes from the north of England and speaks much in that dialect; is very talkative an knock-kneed. From Thomas Price and Thomas Michum in Annapolis, MD. (VG 2 Jun 1774).

Scott, Archibald, about 22, Runaway Scottish Indented Servant said to have gone towards Philadelphia. From Hercules Mulligan, Norfolk, VA. (VG 5 Jan 1775).

Scott, John, about 25, Runaway Servant who served his time with Thomas Johnston; speaks good English with slight lisp. From Zachariah MacCubbin of Annapolis, MD. (VG 1-8 Jun 1739).

Scott, Thomas, no age given, Runaway Scottish Convict Servant, slim made, marked with smallpox, inclined to drinking, speaks much in Scottish dialect and is fond of singing songs, by trade a tailor. From Richard Cadeen in Westmoreland, VA. (VG 28 Jul & 13 Oct 1774).

Screech, William, an elderly man, Runaway Seaman from the ship *Polly* now lying at Bermuda Hundred, VA. From Capt Thomas Duncomb. (VG 11 Jun 1772).

Sears, William, about 20, Runaway Apprentice Boy, house carpenter by trade. From John Gary near Sussex Co Courthouse. (VG 31 Mar 1774).

Self, James, about 25, Runaway Deserter Soldier, corporal of 5th Battalion, Williamsburg, who took part in a mutiny; has a ruddy complexion, brother of William Self (q.v.). From Capt Thomas Gaskins Jr, Williamsburg. (VG 27 Sep 1776).

Self, William, about 23, Runaway Deserter Soldier, corporal of 5th Battalion, Williamsburg, who took part in a mutiny; brother of James Self (q.v.). From Capt Thomas Gaskins Jr, Williamsburg. (VG 27 Sep 1776).

Sellers, Thomas, no age stated, English by birth, Runaway from Col Benjamin Harrison of Charles City Co, VA, Servant of Mrs Stagg, confectioner in Williamsburg, VA, seen going over Chickahominy Bridge in New Kent Co, VA. (VG 6-13 Jan & 12-19 May 1738).

Sharp, Thomas, about 15, [*sentenced at Somerset Quarter Sessions to transportation and landed in Baltimore, MD, in July 1772*], Runaway English Servant. From Benjamin Bradford Norris living near Bush River, Harford Co, MD. (VG 21 Apr 1775).

Shaw, John, no age stated, born in Yorkshire & served his time in Liverpool, blacksmith. From Robert Blackledge of Nansemond Co, VA. (VG 10-17 Jun 1737).

Shaw, John, 18-19, [*sentenced at Southwark Sessions to be transported and shipped to VA in Dec 1771 by the* Justitia], Runaway English Servant with a remarkable scar on his forehead between his eyebrows and scars on his legs. From William Marmaduke near Westmoreland Courthouse, VA. (VG 6 Oct 1775).

Shaw, Robert, no age given, Runaway Scottish Indented Servant who has a long scar on his right arm, appears bold and talks much, by trade a baker. From James Kirk of Alexandria, VA. (VG 17 Jun 1775).

Shepherd, Jane, no age given, Runaway English Servant, lusty fat woman. From Thomas Nevett of Cambridge, Great Choptank River, MD.(VG 15-22 Oct 1736).

Shields, Dennis, about 16, [sentenced at Middlesex Sessions Dec 1765 for stealing silver buckles and transported to VA in Jan 1766 by the Tryal]. Runaway Irish Convict Servant who has been at sea in the East Indies, addicted to lying and loves drinking, by trade a chimney sweep. From John Carlyle at Nomini, VA. (VG 17 Sep 1767).

Shields (Shiels), Robert, about 26, [sentenced at Kent Assizes to be transported and shipped to VA in May 1737 by the Forward], gardener. From Peter Presly, Northumberland Co, VA. (VG 1-17 Nov 1738).

Short, Thomas, middle-aged, Runaway Scottish Seaman from the Encouragement of London lying at West Point, VA. From Alexander Douglas of the said ship. (VG 10 Apr 1752).

Simms, William, Runaway Convict Servant purchased as a farmer or waggoner from Thomas Hodge on board the Scarsdale before escaping from the schooner Occoquan on Rappahannock River; Simms says he was born in Scotland but speaks pretty good English. From Thomas Lawson at Neabsco Furnace, VA. (VG 13 Sep 1770).

Simpson, Alexander (1771) – See Smith.

Simpson, John, no age given, Runaway Servant Boy from the ship Industry laying at Four Mile Creek, James River, VA. From James Lowes, master of said ship. (VG 18 Jan 1770).

Simpson, William, no age given, Runaway English Servant. From Thomas Branson, Stafford, VA. (VG 21 Jul 1768).

Singer, Isaac, no age given, [transported from London Quarter Sessions to VA in Jul 1773 by the Tayloe], Runaway English Convict Servant, thin-faced, small with thin whitish hair. From Archer Matthews living on the levels of Greenbriar, VA. (VG 16 Aug 1776).

Skerum, John, no age given, Runaway Scottish Servant, pretends to be a baker, complicit in the murder of Thomas Horton, skipper of a small schooner returning from Norfolk, VA. From David Galloway of Northumberland C, VA. (VG 19-26 Sep 1745).

Maddall (Smeddle), Richard, no age given, [sentenced in York City & transported in Lent 1766 for stealing in the City],Runaway English Convict Servant about 6 feet tall and marked with smallpox. From H.U. St George of Hog Island, Surry Co, VA. (VG 14 May 1767).

Smith alias Simpson, Alexander, about 30, [sentenced at Middlesex Sessions in Feb 1768 for stealing iron pokers and transported to MD in Apr 1768 by the Thornton], Suspected English Runaway Servant much pitted with smallpox who says he was bred an apothecary and belongs to James Jordan of MD, but at other times that he is a freeman from Philadelphia. From B. Johnston, gaoler of Spotsylvania Co, VA. (VG 20 Jun 1771).

Smith, Charles, no age given, Runaway Mulatto Soldier Deserter, stout with a contracted thumb and forefinger of the left hand. From Sergeant John Sharpe, Williamsburg, VA. (VG 1 Aug 1777).

Smith, Elizabeth, about 25, has very black hair and several scars on her lip, chin and arms and is much pitted by smallpox; she was formerly indented to Capt Gray from Boston, Mass. From Alexander McIntyre in Leesburg, VA. (VG 22 Oct 1772).

Smith, James, about 40, married man living in Isle of Wight Co, VA, who deserted HMS *Hector* in Elizabeth River in 1739. From Yelverton Peyton, Capt of said ship. (VG 2-9 November 1739).

Smith, James, about 20, Suspected Runaway Servant from MD who has a ruddy complexion, now confined in Middlesex Co Gaol, VA. Owner to apply to James Wortham , Sheriff of said Co. (VG 12 Nov 1772).

Smith, James, no age given, Runaway Scottish Convict Servant with remarkable red hair and much freckled in the face. From John McDonald of Goochland, VA. (VG 19 Nov 1772).

Smith, John, about 27, English Runaway Servant who speaks very plain, has a large body and red beard; came in as a schoolmaster. From Thomas Chilton of Westmoreland Co, VA. (VG 24-31 Oct 1745).

Smith, John, no age given, born in Gloucester. Deserter from Capt Thomas Waggoner's Co at Fredericksburg, VA. From Henry Woodward at Fredericksburg. (VG 28 Feb 1755).

Smith, John, no age given, Suspected Runaway Servant who says he belongs to Dr George Stewart in Annapolis, MD, and owns himself a blacksmith. The owner should apply to John Lyne, Gaoler of Frederick Co, MD. (VG 8 Mar 1770).

Smith, Joseph, about 33, Runaway Scottish Servant, very flesh and marked with smallpox, by trade a painter. From Col Fielding Lewis in Fredericksburg, VA. (VG 25 Aug 1775).

Smith, Levin, no age given, Deserter from Capt John Blair's Co of 9th Virginia Regiment when under marching orders. From Lieut Thomas Overton, Williamsburg, VA. (VG 11 Jul 1777).

Smith, Lewis, about 20, Deserter from Capt Crump's 1st Virginia Regiment, born in Brunswick Co and enlisted at York, VA, in Capt Pelham's Co, to be delivered at Williamsburg, VA. From Lieut Matthew Smith. (VG 13 Sep 1776).

Smith, Thomas, no age stated, Runaway Seaman from the *Virginian*, Capt Richard Lewis, at Littlepage's Landing, New Kent Co, VA. (VG 11-18 Apr 1745).

Smith, Thomas, Runaway Indented English Servant, no age given, born in England, carpenter and excellent workman, one of his fingers wounded and a protuberant mouth and nose, fond of spirits. From J Armistead, Williamsburg, VA. (VG 29 Jul 1776).

Smith, William, about 27, [*sentenced at Surrey Assizes in 1772 for stealing a gelding and transported for 14 years to MD in Apr 1772 by the* Thornton], Runaway English Convict Servant, short and well made with sore legs. From John Kidd, Commander of the *Thornton* lying at Leeds Town, VA. (VG 23 Jul 1772).

Smith, William, about 22, Runaway English Convict Servant, well-set, by trade a hatter. From Jonathan Nixon near Bladensburg, Frederick Co, MD. (VG 3 Jun 1773).

Smith, William (1773) – *See* Walker.

Smith, William, about 23, Scotchman who speaks very bad English and is very sickly. He may make for Wilmington, NC, where his brother's widow lived. From John Cockburn, Newcastle, VA. (VG 29 Dec 1774).

Snoock, Joseph, no age given, Runaway English Indented Servant, a labourer. From Robert More, Williamsburg, VA. (VG 16 Nov 1775).

Sole, John, about 19, [possibly the John Soul sentenced to be transported for 14 years at the Gloucester Assizes in Lent 1763], Indented English Servant, shoemaker. From John Apperson, New Kent Co, VA. (VG 24 Feb 1776).

Spain, Isaac, 18, Runaway Apprentice Boy, spare-made. From John Gary near Sussex Co Courthouse. (VG 31 Mar 1774).

Spear, Henry, no age given, of Edgecombe Co, NC, Runaway Soldier Deserter from 3rd Regiment of NC Continental Troops. From Capt James Bradby. (VG 9 May 1777).

Spears, Thomas, about 20, Runaway English Servant born in Bristol, joiner with coarse voice. From George Washington, Fairfax Co, VA. (VG 4 & 12 May 1775).

Spencer, Daniel, about 45, Runaway Irish Servant with a remarkable dent in the middle of his nose and a wen on his belly. From Mark Kenton in Fauquier Co, VA. (VG 11 Oct 1770).

Spicer, Absalom, no age given, apprentice whose parents live in Caroline Co. From Samuel Lomberd, Isle of Wight Co, VA. (VG 16 Apr 1767).

Springett (Springate), William, no age given, [*sentenced at Monmouth Assizes in Lent 1770 to be transported*], Runaway Convict Servant who was born in Wales and bred in Bristol which dialect he speaks, much addicted to drinking and thieving, quarrelsome and abusive; he bears the marks of a recent severe beating he received from breaking into a house, a gardener by trade. From Daniel Chamier, Baltimore, MD. (VG 1 Aug 1771).

Spruce, Absalom, 25-30, [*possibly the Apswell Spruce transported from Middlesex Quarter Sessions by the Justitia to VA in Dec 1769*], Runaway Convict Servant who calls himself a gardener and is awkwardly made with a remarkable thin nose and little marked with smallpox. From Jonathan Boucher in Caroline Co, VA. (VG 16 Aug 1770).

Stanfoot, Francis, no age stated, Suspected Negro Servant who has passed for a freeman, committed to Suffolk Gaol. Apply to gaoler William Granbery. (VG 1 Aug 1771).

Stanton (Staunton) alias Wilson, John, no age given, [*probably the one sentenced in Summer 1773 at Cambridgeshire Assizes to be transported for stealing wheat at Newmarket*], very talkative, pitted with smallpox, by trade a wheelwright. From John Shipard, Williamsburg, VA. (VG 29 Jul 1775).

Staples, Richard, no age given, Runaway Servant who ran from the ship *Becky* in James River, VA, by trade a shipwright much pitted with smallpox who has been seen in Norfolk, VA. From James Buchanan of said ship. (VG 12 Mar 1752).

Steel, John, about 18, [*sentenced Summer 1772 and transported in Jan 1773 from Kent Assizes by the Justitia*], Runaway English Convict Servant, has a much bruised face and very black eyes occasioned by fighting. From Sampson & George Matthews in Richmond, VA. (VG 27 May 1773).

Steel, Joseph, about 30, [*transported from Staffordshire Assizes for 14 years and landed in Baltimore, MD, in Jul 1772*], Runaway English Convict Servant, swarthy with a small scar on his upper lip and ran with an iron ring round his ankle, by trade a hatter. From Jonathan Nixon near Bladensburg, Frederick Co, MD. (VG 3 Jun 1773).

Steale (Steel), William, about 17, [*sentenced Oct 1772 at Middlesex Sessions for stealing a silk coat & transported by the Justitia to VA in March 1773*], Runaway English Convict, a cabinet maker. From Sampson & George Matthews, Richmond, VA. (VG 12 Aug 1773).

Stephens, James, no age given, Runaway Soldier Deserter from 2nd Georgia Battalion who enlisted in Williamsburg, VA. From Lieut Robert Ward, Williamsburg. (VG 24 Jan 1777).

Stevens, William, an elderly man, Runaway Seaman from the ship *Polly* now lying at Bermuda Hundred, VA. From Capt Thomas Duncomb. (VG 11 Jun 1772).

Stewart, Alexander, no age given, Runaway Scottish Deserter who was appointed boatswain of the galley *Hero* and went to Fredericksburg to enlist men but failed to return; he talks broad, is round shouldered and wears an insinuating smile when talking. From John Cockburn, Fredericksburg, VA. (VG 6 Jul 1776.)

Stewart, James, about 25, Scotchman, gardener. From John Mitchell of Urbanna, VA. (VG 16-23 Mar 1739).

Stuart, James, 19, Runaway Apprentice slow of speech and very surly with a roguish look, by trade a wheelwright. From Daniel Hoye of Williamsburg, VA. (VG 30 May 1766).

Stuart, John, 30-35, Runaway Indented Servant with remarkable red eyes who ran from the *Jenny* lying at Broadway, VA. From John Kirkwood of said ship. (VG 2 Jun 1774).

Still, Moses, no age given, [*sentenced Jan 1737 at Dorset Quarter Sessions to be transported to MD & landed in Apr 1738 in Queen Anne's Co, MD, from the Amity*], Runaway Convict Servant, a cooper. From Patrick Creagh, Annapolis, MD. (VG 30 Jun–7 Jul 1738).

Stith, John, no age given, of Bedford, VA, Deserter from Capt Smith's Co of 2nd Georgia Battalion. From Lieut Alexander Baugh of Cumberland Courthouse, VA. (VG 21 Feb 1777).

Stocksdill, William, 17, Deserter from Camp at Maidstone, VA, born in MD. From Commanding Officer, Winchester, VA. (VG 27 Aug 1756).

Stokes, John, about 30, Runaway Virginian Soldier Deserter from 2nd Virginia Regiment in NJ, fond of liquor. From Col Alexander Spotswood of said Regiment. (VG 5 Sep 1777).

Stokes, Young, no age given, Suspected Deserter from Deep Spring Camp, VA, of 6th Virginia Regiment. Warning from Capt James Johnson of said Regt. (VG 30 Aug 1776).

Stone, Henry, no age given, Runaway Servant believed guilty of robbing Josias Cook of Pittsylvania Co, VA. Instruction by John Wilson for him and two others to be apprehended. VG 28 Apr 1775).

Stone, Thomas, no age stated, Runaway Servant, much pox-ridden, tailor by trade. From James Mills, York Town, VA. (VG 10 Jan 1751).

Stossenberg, John Charles, about 27, Runaway Polish deserter from the ship *Berry*, tall and talks in an effeminate way. From James Belcher at Sheppard's Warehouse, Williamsburg, VA. (VG 27 Mar 1752).

Strange, William, no age given, of Brunswick, VA. Deserter from Capt Smith's Co of 2nd Georgia Battalion. From Lieut Alexander Baugh of Cumberland Courthouse, VA. (VG 21 Feb 1777).

Strawther, [first name not given], redheaded and much freckled who lived around Williamsburg, served in the campaign at Norfolk, was discharged but re-enlisted, Runaway Irish Soldier Deserter from 2nd Virginia Regiment in NJ. From Col Alexander Spotswood of said Regiment. (VG 5 Sep 1777).

Stringer, Thomas, about 25, [sentenced at Northamptonshire Assizes for highway robbery Summer 1761 & reprieved for 14 years' transportation in Lent 1762], Runaway Convict Servant with two remarkable moles on his face who speaks fast in the country dialect. From Francis Phillips of Kingsbury Furnace Mine Bank near Baltimore, MD. (VG 29 Sep 1768).

Stringer, William, about 28, [whose brother John Stringer witnessed on his behalf, sentenced at Middlesex Sessions in Sep 1767 for stealing silver tablespoons & transported in Dec 1767 by the *Neptune*], Convict English Servant, who was bought from Thomas Hodge in March 1768 and stole claimant's rum for which he was severely whipped. From Richard Banks of King & Queen Co, VA. (VG 12 May 1768 & 7 Sep 1769).

Stuart – *See* Stewart.

Sturdivant, John, no age given, Runaway Servant missing from Sussex Co, VA, supposedly gone with Isaac Spain and William Sears (q.v.). From John Gary near Sussex Courthouse. (VG 31 Mar 1774).

Sullivane, Margaret (1755) – *See* Connel.

Summers, James, no age given, Runaway Servant from Bristol Co Ironworks, King George Co, VA, a West Country Man who speaks thick. From Hon John Tayloe, Richmond C, VA. (VG 11-19 Mar 1737).

Sumney, Jesse, about 17, Runaway Apprentice from Chesterfield Co, VA, supposedly gone North to board a vessel. From Edmund Graves of Chesterfield Co. (VG 5 Jun 1752).

Sutherland, Daniel, no age given, Runaway Scottish Highland Convict Servant, the only one in his group who speaks English distinctly and ran from the ship *Donald* at Four Mile Creek, Richmond, VA. From James McDowall and Robert Burton in Richmond. (VG 15 Apr 1773).

Swanson, John, about 18, Runaway Apprentice Sailor Lad much pitted with smallpox, a scar burnt on his chest, who speaks broad Yorkshire; he deserted the ship *Brilliant* at Cumberland, VA. From James Miller of said ship. (VG 7 Jul 1774).

Sweney, Edward, 32, Runaway Irish Convict, butcher, well made and with a downcast look, formerly in possession of John Hook, merchant in Bedford NC who sold him to merchants Chambers & Montgomery in Salisbury NC from whom he fled. Owner to approach Peter Pelham, Jailer of Williamsburg, VA. (VG 27 Oct 1774).

Swilavan, Florence, about 30, Runaway Irish Servant Man who will not agree that he can speak English. From Edward Smith of Richmond Town, VA. (VG 14 Feb 1771).

Tailer – *See* Taylor.

Talbot, Henry George, no age given, Suspected Runaway Servant committed to gaol. From Andrew Fleming, Duncan, VA. (VG 23 Feb 1775).

Talbot, Robert, 63, suspected Runaway Servant, 63, says he was born in London. From Thomas Campbell, Gaoler of Winchester, MD. (VG 30 Oct 1766).

Tanker, Mary, no age given, Scotch Servant, runaway with Richard Walsh (q.v.). From William Gay. (VG 19 & 26 Jul 1770).

Tate, Robert, 26-27, Runaway Soldier Deserter from 2nd Battalion recruited in VA for defence of GA, thin-faced, much addicted to liquor, talkative and impertinent when intoxicated. From Lieut John Clarke, Cumberland Co, VA. (VG 7 Mar 1777).

Tate, William, no age given, Runaway Sailor, six feet tall, pitted with smallpox, deserted from the ship *Elizabeth* lying at Alexandria, VA, Capt Frederick Baker. From Robert Adam & Co, Williamsburg, VA. (VG 24 Feb 1775).

Taylor, Drury, about 22, Deserter from the Frontier Battalion at Staunton, Augusta, brother of William Taylor (q.v.), born in VA and whose parents reside in Albemarle Co, VA. From Lieut-Col William Peachey. (VG 30 Nov 1759).

Taylor, Humphrey, about 16, Runaway Scottish Servant Lad, thick and clumsy-made who can neither read nor write. From John Catlett near Aylett's warehouse in King William Co, VA. (VG 9 Feb 1769).

Taylor, Ralph alias Ord, no age given, [*transported for 14 years by Northumberland Assizes in Summer 1735*], North Country Runaway Convict of slow speech. From Patrick Creagh of Annapolis, Md, (VG 8-15 Oct 1736).

Tailer, Samuel, about 19, English Servant, Runaway from sloop *Betsy* at Leeds Town. From Thomas Hodge of Leeds Town, Corotoman River, Lancaster Co, VA. (VG 7 Mar 1771).

Taylor, Thomas, no age given, Runaway English Servant much stooped in his walk with remarkably white teeth, born in Somerset and speaks that dialect. From John Wormeley, Lancaster, VA. (VG 11 Feb 1773).

Taylor, William, 15, Deserter from Camp at Maidstone and the Frontier Battalion at Staunton, Augusta,, VA, born in MD, brother of Drury Taylor (q.v.), Barrott, Mileswhose parents reside in Albemarle Co, VA. From Lieut-Col William Peachey. (VG 30 Nov 1759).

Teal, John (1754) – *See* Towell.

Terelagh, Daniel Connor, Runaway Servant who understands playing the bagpipes. From Miles Barrott, Bedford Co, VA. (VG 18 Mar 1775).

Terrell, James, 21-22, Runaway Servant of Roger Atkinson near Petersburg, VA. From George Cousins of Chesterfield, VA. (VG 7 Mar 1766).

Terrel, John, no age given, Runaway Irish Servant who previously served in MD. From Thomas Ingalls of St Mary's River, MD, joiner. (VG 34-31 Oct 1745).

Tharp, Matthew, no age given, Runaway Irish Convict Servant, well made much pitted with smallpox, by trade a gardener. From Joseph Pierce of Westmoreland Co, VA. (VG 20 Aug , 29 Oct 1772 & 25 Feb 1773).

Thomas, Elizabeth, about 25, [sentenced at London Sessions & transported Dec 1767 by the *Neptune*]. Runaway Welsh Indented Servant, a widow, seen travelling towards Leeds Town, VA. From Francis Peyton of Loudoun Co, VA. (VG 3 Aug 1769).

Thomas, John, no age given, Runaway farmer from the snow *Fortune*, Capt. William Rowntree, lately wrecked in Chesapeake Bay. From George Brown, of Kingston, VA. (VG 5 Oct 1769).

Thomas, William, no age given, Runaway Servant, pretended tumbling-boy supposed to have made for Hampton, VA. From Joseph Barker of Charles Beaver Dams in King George Co, VA. (VG 20 Jun 1751).

Thomas, Winifred, no age stated, [*sentenced at Monmouthshire Assizes for stealing at Bassaleg and awaiting transportation Summer 1736*], Convict Welsh Servant, supposed to have gone to NC. From William Pierce of Nansemond Co, VA. (VG 29 Jul – 5 Aug 1737).

Thompson, Andrew, 17-18, Runaway Irish Lad, somewhat pox marked particularly about the nose. From Peter Cox of Westmoreland Co, VA. (VG 14-21 Oct 1737).

Thompson, Anne, no age given, Runaway Servant of middle size and lusty. From George Woolsey of Norfolk, VA. (VG 8 Feb 1770).

Thompson, Charles, no age given, Runaway Sailor who deserted from the ship *Elizabeth* lying at Alexandria, VA, Capt Frederick Baker. From Robert Adam & Co, Williamsburg, VA. (VG 24 Feb 1775).

Thompson, Francis, no age given, [*sentenced at Yorkshire Assizes for stealing sheep and reprieved to be transported for 14 years in Lent 1771*], Runaway Servant of small size, mean appearance and an arch fellow. From Richard Phillips near Bowler's Ferry, Essex, VA. (VG 31 Oct 1771).

Thompson, James, no age given, Suspected Scottish Convict Servant from Glasgow. Owner to apply to William Granbery, gaoler of Suffolk Gaol, VA. (VG 1 Aug 1771).

Thompson, John, about 18, tall lad born in Blisland, New Kent Co, VA. From William Wyatt, Williamsburg, VA. (VG 25 Aug – 8 Sep 1738).

Thompson, John, 35, (*transported from Southwark Sessions in July 1773 in the* Tayloe], Runaway New England Convict Servant who has a black and surly look and ran from the *Tayloe* at Four Mile Creek, VA. From Sampson & George Mathews, Williamsburg, VA. (VG 11 Nov 1773).

Thompson, William, about 35, Runaway English Servant by trade a bookbinder marked with smallpox. From James Alcorn c/o Patrick Lockhart, merchant in Botetourt, VA. (VG 24 Nov 1774).

Thorpe, Matthew, about 27, Irish Convict Servant seen lately in Richmond Co, VA. From Gilbert Campbell, Westmoreland Co, VA. (VG 17 Jan 1771). Committed to Augusta Co Gaol by Sheriff George Matthews: his owner to pay charges. (VG 9 May 1771).

Thompson, Matthew, no age given, of Bedford Co, VA, Runaway Deserter Recruit raised for the Georgia Service. From Robert & George Walton at Prince Edward Courthouse. (VG 27 Sep 1776).

Thrift, John, no age given, Runaway English Convict Servant (*transported from Surrey Assizes by the Justitia in January 1773*), well-made and with a very impudent look. From Robert McKittrick in Augusta Co, VA, (VG 26 May 1775).

Tippett, John, middle-aged, Runaway Servant who knows something of the carpenter's trade. From Joseph Morton late of Richmond but now of Orange Co, VA. (VG 8-15 Jun 1739).

Tippin, Charles, no age given, Runaway Servant, by trade a gardener and knows a little of the gardener's business. From William Reynolds, Williamsburg, VA. (VG 23 Nov 1775).

Tobin, James, no age given, Suspected Irish Runaway Servant belonging to Capt Somerville committed to Augusta Gaol, VA. Owner to apply to George Matthews, Sheriff of said gaol. (VG 27 Jun 1771).

Todd, Thomas, no age given, Runaway Irish Servant, shoemaker by trade. From William Williams of Culpeper, VA. (VG 11 Apr 1771).

Tolls, Reuben, 23, Runaway Indented Virginia-born Negro Servant who formerly lived in Fredericksburg and plied the ferry between there and Falmouth. From Nicholas Brown Seabrook at Norfolk, VA. (VG 16 Jan 1772).

Tomlins, John, about 26, Runaway Servant, much disfigured with smallpox. From John Lewis of Gloucester Co, VA. (VG 21-28 Apr 1738).

Tomlinson, John, about 35, well-set and a little knock-kneed, RunawaySomerville, Capt English Convict Servant. From Benjamin Howard near Elk Ridge Landing, VA. (VG 18 Jun 1771).

Tomlinson, Samuel, no age given, Runaway Convict Servant, has a sandy beard and is a shoemaker, last seen in New Kent Co, VA. From Thomas William Irwin, in York Town, VA. (VG 12-19 Nov 1736).

Tool, Darby, no age given, Runaway Servant, one-legged and by trade a shoemaker; suspected to have gone to Cherry Point on Potomac in company with Mary Cullen, an Irishwoman he calls his wife. From William Whitehead of Edgcombe Precinct, NC.

Topping (Topin), John, about 55, (transported from London Sessions by the Saltspring in Jul 1775), Runaway English Convict Servant, very bald and without a great toe who is marked with smallpox). From Arthur Edwards in Loudoun Co, VA. (VG 26 Jul 1776).

Towell alias Teal, John, no age given, Runaway Irish Servant from the brig Delight, Capt Bartholomew Rooke. From said Capt Rooke. (VG 7 Nov 1754).

Tracey, Michael, 25, Runaway Irish Indentured Servant, pitted with smallpox and freckled, forward in speech but little of the dialect. From Andrew Wales of Alexandria, Fairfax Co, VA. (VG 26 Jul 1770).

Trap, Thomas, 30, Runaway Sergeant Deserter from 2nd Virginia Regiment in NJ, slim, pitted with smallpox and talks in a whine; he went off with his wife heavy with child. From Col Alexander Spotswood of said Regiment. (VG 5 Sep 1777).

Troop, James, about 23, Deserter from Halifax Regular Co now in Williamsburg. From Capt Nathaniel Cocke. (VG 20 Apr & 10 May 1776).

Trouncer, Samuel, 32, Deserter from HMS Triton, bald headed. From Matthew Whitwell of the said ship. (VG 9 May 1751).

Trump, James, about 26, (transported from Surrey Assizes in 1763 by the Neptune), Runaway Convict Servant, has a scabbed head, by trade a baker. From Robert Adam of Alexandria, Fairfax Co, VA. (VG 6 Jun 1766.

Tucker, Raines, about 17, Runaway Apprentice Boy, by trade a carpenter. From Robert Jones of Southampton Co, VA. (VG 20 Jun 1766).

Tudor, Samuel, about 19, (transported for life from Middlesex Assizes by ship Justitia in 1768), English Convict Servant, runaway from sloop Betsy and belonging to Thomas Hodges of Leeds Town, VA. From Edward Massy of the said sloop. (VG 7 Mar 1771 & 28 Jan 1773).

Turnbull, James, no age given, Runaway Indented Servant who walks very lame, by trade a tailor. From Andrew Hamilton in Blandford, VA. (VG 13 Oct 1774).

Turkel, Thomas, no age given, Runaway English Indented Servant Lad who speaks short and quick, subject to liquor and much pitted with smallpox who ran from on board the sloop Washington lying at Broadway's on Appamattox. From Hillary Moseley of the said vessel. (VG 20 Dec 1776).

Turner, John, no age given, Runaway Servant Boy who ran in Williamsburg, VA. From Darby Skinner of Hampton, VA. (VG 5-12 Nov 1736). From Thomas Nevett of Cambridge, Great Choptank River, MD. (VG 15-22 Oct 1736).

Turner, John, no age given, Runaway English Convict Servant with a club foot which impedes his walking, by trade a shoemaker. From George Donald of Richmond Town, VA. (VG 7 Mar 1766).

Turner, Kinchen, about 25, Deserter from 4th Virginian Battalion in Portsmouth, VA, born in Isle of Wight Co, VA. From Capt Archibald Smith. (VG 20 Sep 1776).

Turpin, Ephraim, 17-18, Runaway Deserter from 7th Regiment of Virginia, court-martialled at Williamsburg, VA, and received 15 lashes. From Charles Fleming of 7th Regt at Gloucester Courthouse, VA. (VG 25 May 1776).

Turtell, Benjamin, no age stated, thick-set country fellow who stole meat and ran off with Brian Cagan (q.v.). Reward offered by Richard Barnes of Richmond Co, VA. (VG 2-9 Jun 1738).

Uleridge, Thomas, no age given, Runaway English Servant pitted with smallpox. From Thomas Branson, Stafford, VA. (VG 21 Jul 1768).

Underwood, John (1774) – See Duberg, Edward.

Usher, John, no age given, (*transported from Durham Quarter Sessions in Lent 1772*), Runaway English Convict Servant, a tall stout fellow from the north of England, rather pale, a weaver by trade who speaks bad English. From James Thompson of the snow *Anne*, Capt Edward Dixon, at Port Royal, VA. (VG 9 Jul 1772).

Valentine, Henry, about 18, Servant born in Leicestershire, about 3 years in this country, speaks very plain, property of Samuel Hipkins of Totuskey Bridge, VA. (VG 25 Aug 1768).

Valentine, Lynde, master of the sloop *Sally*, built in Massachusetts in 1767, who carried off an apprentice James Waters (q.v.) from Pungoteague, VA, and will probably make for a Dutch or Danish port. From Edward Kerr, Accomack, VA. (VG 16 & 23 Apr 1772).

Vaughan, James, about 23, Runaway Deserter from 6th Virginia Regiment at College Camp. From Capt Samuel Cabell. (VG 5 Jul 1776).

Vaughan, Philip, 27, Convict Servant, runaway from Baltimore Ironworks, MD, has a rough face with pimples and a limp, says he has a brother in VA. From Clement Brooke, MD. (VG 15 Jun 1769).

Vest, John. No age given, of Buckingham, VA. Deserter from Capt Smith's Co of 2nd Georgia Battalion From Lieut Alexander Baugh of Cumberland Courthouse, VA. (VG 21 Feb 1777).

Vintjole, Mingo, about 20, speaks bad English, French and Spanish, Runaway Irish Soldier Deserter from Capt de Clovay's Co of French Regiment at Williamsburg, VA. From said Capt de Clovay. (VG 6 Jun 1777).

Waddy, Francis, about 22, Runaway Deserter Soldier of 5th Battalion, Williamsburg, who took part in a mutiny. From Capt Thomas Gaskins Jr, Williamsburg. (VG 27 Sep 1776).

Wade, Joseph, about 40, (*transported for 14 years by the* Thornton *in Apr 1772 from Middlesex Sessions*), Runaway English Convict, short and well-made with his own grey hair; he has been transported four times under different names. From John Kidd, Commander of the *Thornton* lying at Leeds Town, VA. (VG 23 Jul 1772).

Wadling, James(1755) – *See* Wallace.

Wain, Joseph, 22, Runaway Servant who was born in Bucknell, Oxfordshire, round-shouldered with a stooped walk who understands ploughing. From John Mercer of Marlborough, Stafford Co, VA. (VG 6 Jun 1766).

Walbrook. Thomas, no age given, Runaway Servant with John Tippett (q.v.); may be discovered by his lazy disposition. From Joseph Morton late of Richmond but now of Orange Co, VA. (VG 8-15 Jun 1739).

Walke, Anthony, son of Anthony Walke late of Appomattox, VA, no age given, Runaway Servant who stoops and walks awkwardly. From Balfour & Barraud of Norfolk VA. (VG 1 & 3 Nov 1768).

Walker, Adam, about 21, pitted with smallpox. From William Forsyth & Co, Portsmouth, VA. (VG 5 Mar 1772).

Walker, Alice, English Servant who passes for wife of John Eaton (q.v.), and was imported in March 1773 from London Sessions by the *Justitia*, thick and stout-made. From Sampson & George Matthews, Richmond, VA. (VG 12 Aug 1773).

Walker, Robert, 26, Runaway English Convict Servant (*transported from Middlesex Sessions for life by Justitia in Jan 1774*); a member of the ship's company of from the *Justitia* at Leeds Town, Rappahannock who ran with 5 convict servants. From Finlay Gray, Capt of said ship. (VG 24 Mar 1774).

Walker alias Smith, William, no age given, Runaway English Convict Servant who came in the *Scarsdale* in 1771, thin-faced, coarse voice, a remarkable swing in his walk and fond of drink, by trade a gardener. From Richard Lee, Westmoreland, VA. (VG 8 & 12 Jul & 19 Aug 1773).

Wall, John, no age given, Runaway Deserter from Northampton Muster in NC. From Robert Hodgson of Northampton, NC. (VG 27 Jun-3 Jul 1746).

Wallace alias Wadling, James, no age given, Runaway Portuguese Convict Mulatto, a noted pilferer pretending to be a bricklayer and plasterer. From John Brunshill Sr of St Margaret's Parish, Caroline Co, VA. (VG 17 Oct 1755).

Waller, John, about 15, Apprentice of very small growth and talks very fast. From Thomas Llewellyn, Williamsburg, VA. (VG 19 Mar 1772).

Wallner, Isaac, no age given, Runaway Servant who broke gaol in Accomack Co, VA; wheelwright by trade and pretends to be a comb maker, much pox-ridden. From William Beavans, High Sheriff of Accomack Co. (VG 9-16 Sep 1737).

Walsh, Richard, about 23, Indented Irish Servant, frowns when he speaks & pretends to understand ditching and gardening. From William Fleming of Cumberland Co, VA. (VG 19 & 26 Jul 1770).

Walsom, Thomas, about 27, Runaway Convict Servant (*transported for 14 years from Middlesex Sessions by the* Justitia *in Jan 1775*), a little knock-kneed and with a laddish leering look. From Robert Adam, Williamsburg, VA. (VG 17 Jun 1775).

Walters, Walter, about 35, Deserted from Pittsylvania Regular Company in Williamsburg. From Capt Thomas Hutchings, Headquarters, Williamsburg, VA. (VG 24 May 1776).

Walton, Thomas, about 28, Runaway English Convict Servant, a Yorkshireman who speaks bad English. From Edward Stevenson of Little Pipe Creek, Frederick Co, MD.(VG 11 Jun 1767).

Warden, Jesse, no age given, Runaway Marine Deserter from the cruiser *Muskito* lying at Warwick, VA, noted for his great fondness for liquor and troublesome when intoxicated; he may be harboured by his relations in Henrico or Hanover. From Jacob Valentine in Richmond Town, VA. (VG 13 Sep 1776).

Wardrope, John, about 40, Runaway Scottish Indented Servant, thin-faced who speaks the language, a tailor. From Samuel Kempton, Norfolk, VA. (VG 5 Jan 1775).

Warrecker (Warricker), William, about 25, Runaway English Convict Servant (*transported from Middlesex Sessions for 14 years by the* Thornton *in1770*), of a sullen temper, a little bald and much pitted with smallpox. From John Hood Sr and John Hood Jr of Elk Ridge, Anne Arundel Co, MD. (VG 27 Sep1770).

Warren, Christopher, 35, Runaway Irish Servant with a long nose which appears to hang to one side and a few blue spots on his face, a weaver. From George Sell in Frederick Co, VA. (VG 8 Mar 1776).

Wassell, George, about 17, Runaway Indented English Servant much pitted with smallpox, a shoemaker . From Gavin Hamilton, Williamsburg, VA. (VG 17 Jun 1775).

Waters, James, about 19, Runaway Scottish Apprentice bred to the sea, under middle size, thin and short who was taken from Pungoteague , VA, and will probably make for a Dutch or Danish port. From Edward Kerr, Accomack, VA. (VG 16 & 23 Apr 1772).

Waters, Thomas, about 24 but supposedly more, mulatto servant from Liverpool intending for South Carolina. From Thomas Bantam, Sack Point, Nansemond Co, VA. (VG 2-9 May 1745).

Watkins, Henry, no age given, Welsh Runaway Servant. From William Hobday of York Co, VA. (VG 12-19 May 1738).

Watkinson, William, no age given, English Servant last seen heading for Northumberland Co, VA. From John Turberville, Westmoreland Co, VA. (VG 3 & 17 Nov 1768).

Watson alias Stewart, Elizabeth, about 40, (*transported from Middlesex Sessions by the* Essex in 1740). Runaway Convict Servant who says she is not more than 32 and has 14 children; she was born in

Ireland but may pretend her birthplace was St Andrew's, Holborn, London. From Charles Julian of Fredericksburg, VA. (VG 10 Jul 1752).

Watson, James, 20, Runaway Scottish Convict Servant (*transported from London Sessions by the Justitia in Jan 1774*). From Capt Finlay Gray of the said ship at Leeds Town, Rappahannock, VA. (VG 24 Mar 1774).

Watson, James, about 20, Suspected Runaway Irish Convict Servant who is quite deaf and claims to be servant to John Wayman in MD. Advertiser James Gordon in Williamsburg says this man (the same as the James Watson above?) came to his house in Aug 1775. (VG 9 Nov 1775).

Watson, William, 30-35, Suspected Runaway Yorkshire Servant, very impudent and talkative who says "he lived with John Gunyon in Dumfries, VA, but seems closely to fit the description of John Booker (q.v.)" advertised by James Duncanson. From Richard Barnett, Gaoler of Westmoreland Co, VA. (VG 8 Oct 1772).

Watts, John, about 26, Runaway English Convict Servant, a shoemaker by trade, remarkably fond of liquor. (*transported by the* Scarsdale *from Hertfordshire Quarter Sessions in 1770*). From John Gardener, King and Queen Co, VA, 14 Feb 1771).

Weakly, Susanna, no age given, Runaway Servant, lusty wench speaking with a North of England dialect who says she was born in Lincolnshire. From John Silbey of Stafford Co, VA. (VG 27 Jun-4 Jul 1745).

Weathered, Anthony, no age stated, Runaway Servant who was condemned but pardoned for a felony and is supposed to have gone towards Lunenberg, VA, or NC. From John Lane, Williamsburg, VA. (VG 8 Aug 1751).

Webb, Mary, no age given, Runaway mantua maker from the snow *Fortune*, Capt. William Rowntree, lately wrecked in Chesapeake Bay. From George Brown, of Kingston, VA. (VG 5 Oct 1769).

Webb, William, no age given, apprentice boy tailor, probably heading for Roanoke, VA. From Charles Coppedge near Stony Creek, Dinwiddie Co, VA. (VG 10 Nov 1768).

Webster, William, over 30, Runaway Scottish Servant, brickmaker who talks pretty broad. From George Washington, Fairfax Co, VA. (VG 4 & 12 May 1775).

Webster, William, 23, Runaway English Servant, thin faced with thin lips who is parrot-toed and a forward talkative fellow, a hatter by trade. From William Reynolds, Williamsburg, VA. (VG 23 Nov 1775).

Wells, Richard, no age given, Runaway English Servant of low stature who shaves and bleeds well and has razors and lancets with him; he also reads and writes well. From John Norton, Goose Creek, Loudoun Co, VA. (VG 9 Jan 1772).

Wells, Samuel, about 25, Runaway who helped steal a schooner at Sappelo Island, Georgia, the property of Patrick Mackay; the pirate is tall and slim and was born in Rhode Island. From the said Mackay. (VG 13 Jan 1776).

Wells, William, no age given, Runaway English Convict Servant imported in Spring 1775 in the *Justitia*, very thin a little marked by smallpox and a somewhat red nose; very saucy and fond of liquor (*transported from Essex Assizes by sentence of Lent 1774*). From Francis Christian in Farnham Parish, Richmond Co, Va.

Welsh, James, about 25, Runaway Indentured Servant belonging to Thomas Carter of Duncan, Norfolk, VA, much addicted to liquor, with three scars between his eyebrows. From Thomas Rowand, Lancaster Co, VA. (VG 28 Jul 1774).

Welsh, James, no age given, Runaway Indented Irish Servant, slim, addicted to liquor and quarrelsome when drunk; is believed to have gone towards NC. From William Forsyth, Norfolk Co, VA. (VG 5 Jul 1775).

Welsh, Thomas, about 21, Runaway Irish Servant, about 21, speaks bad English. From Samuel Ingram, nine miles from English Ferry on New River, VA. (VG 30 Jun 1775).

Westan, Nicholas, about 23, born in Yorkshire and pitted with smallpox. Runaway Servant who came in as a book-keeper but served as a schoolmaster. From Taverner Beal of Orange Co, VA. (VG 11 Apr 1755).

Weston, George, no age given, Runaway Soldier Deserter from Capt Charles Tomkies' Co of 7th Regiment and probably now in Gloucester Co, VA, where it was raised. From Reuben Lipscomb, Williamsburg, VA. (VG 24 Jan 1777).

Wharton (Warton), Thomas, 18, Runaway English Convict Servant born at Hackney near London, a little pitted with smallpox, who was purchased on board the *Justitia* near Leeds Town, Rappahannock River in February 1772, (*transported from Middlesex Sessions in Dec 1771*). From A. Hamilton, of Petsworth parish, Gloucester Co, VA. (VG 9 Apr 1772).

Whatmore, John, about 21, young looking house joiner who ran from the ship *Chance*, Capt Campbell. From Brown, Grierson & Co, Norfolk, VA. (VG 12 Aug 1773).

Whealon, Daniel, 30, Irish Convict, smith belonging to Abraham Bedel, Hanover Co, VA, and formerly to John Fitzgerald of King William Co. From William Parks, Hanover Courthouse, VA. (VG 5-12 Dev 1745).

Wheatley, Anne, no age given, Runaway Convict Servant, no age given, lusty and well set, a Londoner transported by *Dorsetshire* to VA in 1736. From Francis Smith, Essex Co, VA. (VG 11-18 Nov 1737).

White, Adam, no age stated, Runaway Apprentice. From Walter Lenox of Williamsburg, VA. (VG 10 Aug 1769).

White, Charles, about 28, (*probably sentenced at Middlesex Quarter Sessions in1773 to be transported*), Runaway English Convict in Frederick Co, VA, by trade a stocking weaver, born in Rutlandshire, pug-nosed, who ran from Marlborough Ironworks; twice escaped and apprehended From Isaac Zane of Marlborough, Frederick Co, VA. (VG 23 Nov 1775, 29 Jun, 22 & 29 Nov 1776).

White, Daniel, no age given, Runaway Sailor with a defect in one eye who deserted the ship *Fairfield* now lying at Norfolk, VA. From Capt Gawin Hamilton. (VG 3 Jan 1771).

White, James, about 26, Runaway Deserter from HMS *Fowey* in Hampton Road, VA. From Policarous Taylor, Commander of said ship. (VG 3-10 Oct 1745).

White, James, no age given, Runaway Soldier Deserter from Capt Charles Tomkies' Co of 7th Regiment and probably now in Gloucester Co, VA, where it was raised. From Reuben Lipscomb, Williamsburg, VA. (VG 24 Jan 1777).

White, John, no age stated, Runaway Indented Servant of cheerful countenance who came from Berwick and speaks in the north country dialect; he professes gardening and farming. From John Kilty living near Layn's Creek in Anne Arundel Co, MD. (VG 7 Jul 1774).

White, Robert Tate, formerly living with David White near Richmond, VA, now suspected Runaway Soldier Deserter from an Artillery Co in which he enlisted. From William Pierce Jr, Williamsburg. (VG 28 Mar & 13 Jun 1777).

Whitehurst, Levi, no age given, of Princess Anne Co, VA, Runaway Soldier Deserter from 15th Continental Battalion. From Capt William Grimes, Williamsburg, VA. (VG 28 Mar 1777).

Whitley (Wheatley), Anne, about 30, Londoner transported in 1736 by the *Dorsetshire* to VA. From Francis Smith of Essex Co, VA. (VG 20-27 Jan & 11-18 Nov 1737).

Whittaker, Abraham, 19, born in Md, Deserter from Camp at Maidstone, VA. From Commanding Officer, Winchester, VA. (VG 27 Aug 1756).

Whittaker, Isaac, 21, Deserter from Camp at Maidstone, VA, born in MD. From Commanding Officer, Winchester, VA. (VG 27 Aug 1756).

Wigginton, Margaret, no age given, Runaway from the snow *Fortune*, Capt. William Rowntree, lately wrecked in Chesapeake Bay. From George Brown, of Kingston, VA. (VG 5 Oct 1769).

Wigginton, Robert, no age given, Runaway turner from the snow *Fortune*, Capt. William Rowntree, lately wrecked in Chesapeake Bay. From George Brown, of Kingston, VA. (VG 5 Oct 1769).

Wignall, Francis, about 25, Runaway Convict Servant, by trade a shoemaker. From Robert Adam of Alexandria, Fairfax Co, VA. (VG 6 Jun 1766).

Wilcocks, John, 21, Runaway English Convict Servant with a sickly look and a cough. From Edward Stevenson of Little Pipe Creek, Frederick Co, MD.(VG 11 Jun 1767).

Wilkins, Robert of Henrico, VA, no age given, Deserter from Capt Smith's Co of 2nd Georgia Battalion. From Lieut Alexander Baugh of Cumberland Courthouse, VA. (VG 21 Feb 1777).

Wilkinson, George, Runaway English Convict Servant (*transported from Middlesex Sessions in 1765 by the* Neptune), about 20 with red hair. From Robert Whitley and John Maxwell in forks of James River, Augusta Co, VA. (VG 16 Jun 1768).

Wilkinson, John, no age given, Runaway Servant, thin faced and surly looking, by trade a gardener. From William Lightfoot of Tedlington, VA. (VG 24 Jan 1752).

Will, Lauchlane, no age given, Runaway Scottish Highland Convict Servant who ran from the ship *Donald* at Four Mile Creek, Richmond, VA, in his own country garb. From James McDowall and Robert Burton in Richmond. (VG 15 Apr 1773).

Williams, Andrew, about 27-28, with scarce any beard, a noted villain who speaks a west of England dialect and may well try to pass himself off as a soldier. Escaped Convict from John R Holliday, Sheriff of Baltimore, MD. (VG 1 Aug 1771).

Williams, Anthony, 25-26, Runaway Indented Servant of Monmouthshire, middle-sized, by trade a tailor. From William Binsley, Master of the snow *Castle* lying at York Town, VA. (VG 19 May 1774).

Williams, Christopher, about 25, Runaway Irish Servant who speaks plain and can write. From John Mountjoy, Stafford, VA. (VG 23 Apr 1772).

Williams, Edward, no age given, Runaway English Convict Servant (*transported from London Sessions by the* Justitia *in 1767*). From Robert Phillips at Fredericksburg, VA. (VG 28 Jan 1768).

Williams, Edward, about 30, Runaway Welsh Servant who speaks the dialect. From Abraham Jarrett, Baltimore, MD. (VG 4 Aug 1774).

Williams, John, no age given, Servant from the West Country. From William Richards of Drysdale parish, King & Queen Co, VA. (VG 8-15 Jun 1739).

Williams, John, no age given, Runaway English Convict Servant, thick well-set with a brazen look with several warts on his hands and a remarkable scar under his nose; he formerly taught at a reading school in Prestonburg; is likely to pass as a deserter from General Gage. From Henry Williams in Prestonburg, Pittsylvania Ca, VA. (VG 4 Aug 1775).

Williams, John, no age given, talks hoarse, much pitted with smallpox, shipped from 8th Regiment as seaman in cruiser *Revenge*, Capt William Deane. Runaway from Aaron Jeffery, Cumberland Co, VA. (VG 19 Jul 1776).

Williams, John, no age given, Deserter from Capt Smith's Co of 2nd Georgia Battalion who served under Capt Morgan Alexander. From Lieut Alexander Baugh of Cumberland Courthouse, VA. (VG 21 Feb 1777).

Williams, John, no age given, Suspected Runaway Soldier Deserter who enlisted at Jamestown, VA. From William Pierce Jr, Williamsburg, VA. (VG 28 Mar & 13 Jun 1777).

Williams, Peter, 20, Deserter from Camp at Maidstone, VA, born in MD. From Commanding Officer, Winchester, VA. (VG 27 Aug 1756).

Williams, Richard, no age given, Runaway Welsh Servant belonging to Samuel Washington who will pass for a sailor or gardener. From John Champe of King George Co, VA. (VG 11 Apr 1755).

Williams, William, about 23, Runaway Indented Servant who has served for four years, speaks with a Scottish accent, a baker by trade, no age given, left the ship *Elizabeth* lying at Alexandria, VA, Capt Frederick Baker. From Robert Adam & Co, Williamsburg, VA. (VG 24 Feb 1775).

Willis, Moses, Runaway Waggoner much used to travelling in the back parts as a freeman. From Edward Travis on Poplar Creek, Brunswick Co, VA. (VG 25 Aug 1774).

Willmore alias Willmott, Sarah, about 23, Runaway Servant who has a little of the Irish brogue but denies that country, has a pert impudent look and is pox-ridden. From Robert Vaulx of Westmoreland Co, Potomac, VA. (VG 2 Mat 1751).

Wilmore, William, no age given, Runaway English Convict Servant who has lost a thumb, a short man much given to flattery and laughter, a weaver by trade. From John Marr in Pittsylvania, VA. (VG 15 Jun 1775).

Wilmott, Ambrose, no age given, Runaway drawer from the snow *Fortune*, Capt. William Rowntree, lately wrecked in Chesapeake Bay. From George Brown, of Kingston, VA. (VG 5 Oct 1769).

Willmott, Sarah (1751) – *See* Willmore.

Wills, William, about 20, Runaway Apprentice supposedly gone to NC. From Thomas Brewer of York Town, VA. (VG 27 Jun-3 Jul 1746).

Wilson, Charles, no age given, of Halifax Co, VA, Runaway Deserter Recruit raised for the Georgia Service. From Robert & George Walton at Prince Edward Courthouse. (VG 27 Sep 1776).

Wilson, Edward, about 18, Runaway Mulatto Apprentice Lad who has a scar on his right foot caused by an axe blow; he is supposed to have gone towards Hampton, VA. From Philip Mallory of Mecklenburg, VA. (VG 5 Sep 1771).

Wilson, George, 19, Deserter from Camp at Maidstone, VA, born in MD. From Commanding Officer, Winchester, VA. (VG 27 Aug 1756).

Wilson, Hannah, about 50, (*perhaps transported from Middlesex Sessions in* 1754), born in Denmark but speaks Low Dutch and good English, Runaway Servant supposed to have gone away with some sailors rejoining their ship at Hampton, VA. From Henry Brinker of Winchester, Frederick Co. VA. (VG 5 Sep 1755).

Wilson, John alias John William, no age given. Runaway Servant from Yorkshire, professed ploughman and ditcher. From Zachariah Hicks of Bull Hill, Appamattox River, Prince George Co, VA. (VG 13-20 Apr 1739).

Wilson, John (1775) – *See* Stanton.

Wilson, John, no age given, Runaway Soldier Deserter from 2nd Georgia Battalion who enlisted in Williamsburg, VA. From Lieut Robert Ward, Williamsburg. (VG 24 Jan 1777).

Wilson, Peter, about 24, Indented Scottish Servant, round shouldered, speaks broad and has a very down look, a butcher by trade, a good ostler and weaver. From John Syme, Newcastle, VA. (VG 2 Aug 1775).

Wilson, Sarah (1752) – *See* Knox.

Winn, James, no age stated, Suspected Deserter soldier runaway from Deep Spring Camp, VA, of 6th Virginia Regiment. Warning from Capt James Johnson of said Regt. (VG 30 Aug 1776).

Winthrop, Thomas, about 25, (*transported from Lancaster Assizes in 1768*), Runaway English Convict Servant born in Carlisle, Yorks, round-shouldered, stooped and has a reddish beard; he escaped wearing an iron collar. From George Kellor of Frederick Co, VA. (VG 20 Jul 1769).

Witmore, Henry, no age given, Runaway Servant, slim. From Edward Stevenson, Little Pipe Creek, Frederick Co, MD. (VG 12 Mar 1772).

Wolley, William, about 27, Runaway English Indented Servant imported this fall in the *Lord Camden*, Capt John Johnstoun, from London; shows his teeth when he speaks and has a thin visage, belongs to Richard Henry Lee of Westmoreland Co, VA. From Daniel Morgan of Westmoreland Co. (VG 8 Nov 1770).

Wood, John, about 22, (*transported from Middlesex Sessions in 1772*), Runaway English Convict Servant thick well-set fellow, very full faced, speaks very plain and pitted with smallpox, by trade a bricklayer. From John Howlett in Urbanna, Gloucester Co, VA. (VG 4 Mar 1773).

Wood, Robert, about 18, Runaway English Servant who has broken right wrist, weaver by trade, now thought to be in Prince George Co, VA. From Thomas Robins, Gloucester Co, VA. (VG 23 Sep 1773).

Wood, Robert, 30, Runaway English Convict Servant born in the north of England and pitted with smallpox, transported by the *Justitia* from London in Jan 1774. From Capt Finlay Gray of the said ship at Leeds Town, Rappahannock, VA. (VG 24 Mar 1774).

Wood, William, 22, born in London, pitted with smallpox, plays a little on the fife, Runaway Seaman who deserted the sloop of war *American Congress* in Yeocomico, Northumberland Co, VA. From John Allison, Capt of Marines of said vessel. (VG 21 Jun 1776).

Wood, William, no age given, Runaway Deserter Soldier from 1st Regiment, born in Elizabeth City Co and believed now to be in Capt Calvert's galley. From Capt Edmund B Dickinson of said Regiment. (VG 16 Aug 1776).

Worsham, Charles, aged 17-18, Runaway Apprentice. From Thomas Davis, Amelia Co, VA, tailor. (VG 15 Feb 1770).

Wright, John, about 24, Runaway Servant, glazier by trade, who ran from the ship *Walpole* in James River. From William Parks, Printing Office, Williamsburg, VA. (VG 6-13 Oct 1738).

Wright, John, about 24, Runaway Scottish Convict Servant who has sailed out of London for 12 years and was transported to MD in the *Douglas*, Capt Brackenridge in Oct 1769 but ran away in the next month. From John G Frazer of West Point, King William Co, VA. (VG 7 Dec 1769).

Wright, Sugar, no age given, Suspected Deserter from Deep Spring Camp, VA, of 6th Virginia Regiment. Warning from Capt James Johnson of said Regt. (VG 30 Aug 1776).

Wyat, John, no age stated, West Country man who broke gaol in Accomack Co, VA; pretends he lives at Piscataway, New England, and is supposed to have gone towards Hampton, VA. From William Beavans, High Sheriff of Accomack Co. (VG 9-16 Sep 1737).

Wylie, John, 20, Runaway Irish Servant with a very bumpy face who speaks pretty plain and betrays his nationality thereby. From James Craig of Lunenburg Co, VA. (VG 1 Jun 1769).

Yorke, John, about 22, (*probably transported from Surrey Assizes by the* Justitia *in 1767*), Runaway English Servant with a mole on his left eyebrow. From Robert Gilkison & David Hogshead near Jennings' Gap, Williamsburg, VA. (VG 27 Oct 1768).

Young, Andrew, 30, Runaway Convict Servant, an impudent fellow who is pox-marked. From Patrick Coutts on James River, Richmond, VA. (VG 16 May 1766).

Young, Daniel, Convict Servant six feet tall, no age given. From Daniel Hornby, Richmond Co, VA. (VG 4-11 May 1739).

Young, John, no age given, Runaway English Servant who ran before and was taken up at Port Royal, VA; he lisps and stoops much when he walks. From Jacob Brake on the South Fork of the South Branch in Hampshire Co, VA. (VG 18 Mar 1775).

Supplementary Runaways Index

Name	Pages	Name	Pages
Adam, Robert	18,23,29,80,83,86,89,91	Barnes, Capt Joseph	22
Adams, Richard	10	Barnes, Joseph	3,32*
Alcorn, James	82	Barnes, Richard	12,67,84,87
Alderson, Jeremiah	1	Barradall, Edward	21
Alexander, Capt Morgan	90	Barrott, Miles	81
Alexander, Jesse	33	Barry, Edward	5
Alexander, William	39	Bartlett, William	1
Allan, James	34	Barton, John	34
Allan, William	25	Batchelor, Peter	3
Allen, George	2	Battersby, W	73
Allen, Hugh	19,34,45	Baugh, Lieut Alexander	24,47,50,78,79,84,89,90
Allen, John	2	Beal, Taverner	88
Allen, Randall	46	Beavans, William	85,93
Allinsord, Philip	39	Beavars, William	49,68
Allison, Capt John	5,7,58,63,92	Beckwith, Roger	3
Anderson, James	11	Bedel, Abel	88
Anner, Robert	57	Beedles, Robert	48
Apperson, John	77	Belcher, James	10,56,79,
Arell, Richard	8,60	Belches, James	45
Arell, Samuel	9,50	Bell, William	18,67
Armistead, J	76	Benger, Dorothea	29
Armistead, Thomas	62	Benhan, John	6
Armston, Freer	28	Benn, James	53
Armstrong, Capt	34	Berry, Richard	7
Armstrong, James	54	Berryman, Benjamin	37
Aseren, Thomas	38	Binsley, William	28,52,90
Atkinson, James	37,56	Birmingham, Mr	72
Atkinson, John	17,25,54	Bissitt, Alexander	43
Atkinson, Roger	81	Black, William	10,20,35
Attwell, Thomas	67	Blackburn, Col	60
Austin, William	69	Blackburn, Thomas	31
Avery, Lieut Billey H	37	Blackledge, Robert	74
Aylett, John	36,38*	Blair, Capt John	12,15,46,64,76
Aylett, William	14	Blanchard, John	68,69
Aylett, William	53	Bland, John	1
Bailey, Josiah	3	Blincoe, Thomas	22,60
Baird, John	61	Blyth, William	4,37
Baker, Capt Frederick	29,70,80,81,91	Boaten, Lewis	51
Baker, Edward	69	Boatman, Richard	57
Baker, Richard	55	Bodeley, Matthias	53
Balfour & Barraud	85	Bond, Buckler	10,64
Ball, John	69	Bond, Thomas	18
Ball, Mr	70	Bordland, Mrs	10
Ballendine, John	25	Bordland, Mary	24
Ballendine, Mrs	59	Botkin, John	48
Banks, Richard	79	Boucher, Rev.	14
Bantam, Thomas	86	Boucher, Jonathan	50,77
Barker, Joseph	81	Boush, Samuel	35
Barkley, William	1	Bowers, Peter	61
Barnaby, Elias	36	Bowyer, John	39
Barnes, Col	33	Boyd, David	58

Supplementary Runaways Index

Name	Pages	Name	Pages
Boyd, James	11	Campbell, John	16
Brackenridge, Capt	93	Campbell, Thomas	71,80
Bradby, Capt James	30,33,41,45,77	Canaday, John	48
Bradby, James	7	Canby, Samuel	43,49
Braddock, General	8,41,52	Carlyle, John	44,75
Bradley, Capt	33	Carr, William	6
Brake, Jacob	93	Carrol, Charles	41
Branson, Thomas	75,84	Carter, Charles	17,31,50
Brenon, John	61	Carter, Hon John	65
Brent, William	8,54	Carter, John	51
Brewer, Thomas	91	Carter, Landon	62
Briden, James	18	Carter, Samuel	32
Briggs, William	19	Carter, Thomas	88
Brinker, Henry	91	Cassay, Philip	25
Brittan, John	13	Castillo, Bridget	65
Brockenbrough, John	68	Catlett, John	21,80
Brooke, Clement	14,84	Catton, Benjamin	11,14
Brooke, Humphry	37	Causin, Gerard B	22
Brooke, Dr Richard	14	Cawley, John	1
Brown Grierson & Co	26,33,88	Chambers & Montgomery	52,56,72,80
Brown, Francis	16	Chambers, John	34
Brown, George	16,19,21,26,30,32,40,60,68,72,73,81,87,89*,91	Chamier, Daniel	77
		Champe, John	6,73,90
Brown, James	2	Chancey, William	4,35
Brown, John	32	Chapman, Nathaniel	2,74
Brown, William	60	Charlock, Nicholas	15
Brunshill, John Sr	85	Chesley, Robert	52
Buchanan, Capt	51	Chew, Capt Nathaniel	45
Buchanan, Mr	24	Chilton, Thomas	76
Buchanan, James	18,78	Chiswell, Charles	53
Buckland, William	4,28	Chiswell, John	53
Bucktrout, Benjamin	21	Christian, Francis	88
Burd, Andrew	45	Churchill, Armistead	44
Burnley, Lieut Garland	49	Clarke, Lieut John	2,36,80
Burton, Lieut-Col	8	Clay, Perciball	16
Burton, Robert	27*,56,57,80,90	Clifton, Thomas	11
Burwell, Lewis	40	Clopton, George Jr	20
Bushrode, John	31,52,55	Cockburn, John	77,78
Butler, John	17	Cocke, Joseph	41
Butler, Thomas	41	Cocke, Capt Nathaniel	8,22,23,40,52,83
Byrd, William	8,59	Cockil, John	16
Cabell, Capt Samuel	84	Cocks, Thomas	63
Cabell, Capt Samuel Jordan	5,13	Cole, Richard	41
Cadeen, Richard	74	Coleman, Henry	43
Cagan, Brian	67,84	Coleman, John	60
Callaway, John	29	Coleman, Robert	1
Calvert, Capt	92	Collier, Lieut Charles	30
Calvert, John	14	Collins, George	9
Campbell, Capt	26,33,48,88	Colloney, Richard	61
Campbell, Gilbert	82	Colvard, Benjamin	12,70
Campbell, James	38,58,	Combs, John	59
Campbell, James	62		

Supplementary Runaways Index

Name	Page
Commodore, John	41
Connel, Margaret	79
Cook, Josias	31,62,79
Coppedge, Charles	87
Corries, John	36
Cosby, William	55
Cousins, George	81
Coutts, Patrick	34,58,93
Cox, Peter	81
Craig, James	93
Crawford, Andrew	19
Creagh, Patrick	15,17,57,78,80
Crenshaw, John	33,43
Critendon, Hannah	2
Crop, James Jr	11
Cross, Joseph	55
Crow, James	5
Cubbin, Andrew	46,61
Cullen, Mary	83
Currier, David	49
Curtis, Christopher	10
Custis, John Parke	20,67
Dalton, John	10
Dames, John	20
Dames, William	37
Danby, John	45
Dandridge, N.N.	3
Daniel, Edward	56
Daniel, Reuben	39
Daniel, Samuel	40,72
Dansie, Capt	36
Dansie, Thomas	42
Darling, Capt John	71
Dashiell, Joseph	53
Davies, Lieut John R	62
Davis, Mary	64
Davis, Thomas	92
Davis, William	9,61
De Clovay, Capt	84
De Graffenreid, Tsb	42
Deakins, William	73
Deane, Capt William	13,90
Deane, Elkanah	43,67
Deverix, James	23
Dick, Alexander	70
Dick, Charles	55
Dickerson, David	23
Dickinson, Capt Edmund B	92
Diggens, Daniel	26
Divers, George	12,70
Dixon, Capt Edward	27,84
Dobby, James	23
Dobson, Robert	40
Donald, George	10,84
Donally, William	10
Dorell, Sampson	28
Douglas, Alexander	44,49,58,75
Dowman, Rawleigh	51
Draper, John	45
Drybrow, Thomas	25
Duberg, Edward	84
Dudley, Capt Robert	53
Duff, Arthur	25
Dunbar, Col	52
Duncanson, James	8,25,50,87
Duncomb, Capt Thomas	74,78
Dunmore, Lord	31
Dupree, John	29
Durfey, Francis	40
Duval, Samuel	34,43
Eaton, John	26
Edmondson, James	31
Edwards, Arthur	83
Ellyson, Gerard	65
Emens, Joseph	2
Emerson, James	51,53,72
Esten, James	62
Evans, Francis	66
Everee, John	3
Evrie, John	3
Ewin, John	27
Falmouth, John	50
Farr, Samuel	30*
Faw, Abraham	5
Fearson, William	31
Fendall, Benjamin	39
Ficklin, William	48,60
Field, Thomas	49
Findly, James	62
Finnie, Capt Alexander	63
Fitzgerald, John	30,72
Fitzhugh, Thomas	35
Fitzjarrel, Morris	47
Fleming, Lieut	36
Fleming, Andrew	80
Fleming, Charles	37,84
Fleming, Gardner	56
Fleming, Henry	50
Fleming, William	86
Flodd, Patrick	14
Flood, Dr William	37
Flood, William	18

Supplementary Runaways Index

Forsyth, William	10,85,88	Griffin, LeRoy	9,59
Foster, William	59	Griffis, Thomas	12
Fox, Nathaniel	62	Griffith, Charles G	23,46
Franklin, James	53	Griffith, Henry Jr	23,33,46
Frazer, John G	71,93	Grigg, Capt	20
Freeman, William	10	Grimes, Capt William	28,47,64,89
French, James	36,59	Grimes, Maximillian	16
Fryatt, Bartholomew	59	Grymes, Benjamin Jr	21
Fryer, Capt	66	Grymes, H	4,27
Fryet, Bartholomew	31	Grymes, Philip	61
Furr, Ephraim	4	Gunyon, John	87
Gage, General	90	Haden, Anthony	18
Gaine, Hugh	53	Hague, Francis	28
Gaines, Harry	11,59	Hall, Henry	8
Gaines, Henry	8	Hall, Lieut John	9
Galloway, David	44,75	Hall, Philip	54
Galloway, Joseph	19	Hall, William	35
Gamble, Richard	73	Halpin, John	73
Gardener, James	8,15	Hamilton, A	88
Gardener, John	87	Hamilton, Andrew	24,83
Garlick, Samuel	50	Hamilton, Gavin	29,86
Garretson, Job	70	Hamilton, Capt Gawin	89
Gary, John	74,77,79	Hamilton, Gawin	58
Gasford, Samuel	14	Hamilton, Thomas	64
Gaskins, Capt Thomas	74*,85	Hammond, Charles	49,70
Gaskins, Capt Thomas Jr	20	Hammond, Charles Jr	20
Gay, William	80	Hanson, Samuel	6,57
Geddy, James	48	Harn, James	37
Geoghegan, Anthony	73	Harper, Margaret	1
Gibson, James	44	Harpiron, Mr	38
Gilkison, Robert	68,93	Harrington, James	36
Gillam, Joseph	24	Harris, John	19,41,72
Gist, Mordecai	15,34	Harris, Samuel	42
Golat, John	60	Harris, William	3
Gooch, William	6,23,29	Harrison, Col Benjamin	74
Gordon, John	87	Harrison, Capt Carter	69
Gorsuch, John	40	Harrison, Col Nathaniel	69
Graham, George	38	Harvey, Mungo	71
Graham, James	1,27,30	Harwood, Humphrey	40,46
Graham, Reginald	61	Hatfield, Richard	38
Graham, Richard	25,66	Hatton, William	38,43
Granbery, William	77,82	Hayth, William	47
Granger, Francis	33	Hazlegrove, John	68
Grant, Daniel	14	Headen, John	38
Grattan, John	45,49	Henderson, Alexander	39
Graven, Morgan	22	Hendrick, Zachariah	55
Graves, Edmund	79	Herne, Peeling	41
Green, Richard	43	Herriford, John	2
Green, Thomas	4,24	Herriter, Casper	48
Greenbury, Charles	33	Hicklen, Hugh	69
Gresham, William	19	Hicks, Zachariah	29

Supplementary Runaways Index

Name	Pages	Name	Pages
Higgin, James	34,56	Inglis & Long	33,36,44,71
Hill, Edward	21,33,58	Ingram, Samuel	88
Hilldrup, Samuel	7	Innis, James	34
Hipkins, John	20	Irwin, Thomas William	83
Hipkins, Samuel	65,84	Jackson, Capt Benjamin	50
Hobday, John	23	Jackson, Robert	5
Hobday, William	66,86	Jackson, William Jr	37
Hobson, Nicholas	20,64	James, Henry	15,34
Hodge, Thomas	2,51,69,75,79,80,83	James, Micajah	14
Hodgson, Robert	85	Jameson, David	38
Hoffman, Peter	5	Jarrett, Abraham	66,90
Hogshead, David	68,93	Jeffery, Aaron	13,90
Holebreech, Mr	11	Jeffries, Samuel	65
Holliday, John R	90	Jenkins, William	43
Hollingshaw, Michael	41	Jerman, Stephen Jr	7
Holloway, James	70	Johnson, Andrew	31,63
Holmes, Edward	30	Johnson, Capt James	8,12,15,17,41,42,45,79,92,93
Holmes, William	12	Johnson, James	32
Holshaw, Michael	41	Johnson, John	41
Holt, John	44	Johnston, B	3
Holt, Richard Jr	58	Johnston, Benjamin	61
Homes, John	37	Johnston, Capt John	16
Hood, John Jr	43,86	Johnston, John	10
Hood, John Sr	43,86	Johnston, John B	75
Hood, John	69	Johnston, Richard	64
Hook, John	30,56,72.80	Johnston, Stephen	61
Hopkins, Samuel	65	Johnston, William	62
Horbert, Thomas	39	Johnstoun, Capt John	92
Hornby, Daniel	4,24,47,93	Jones, Robert	83
Horton, Thomas	44,75	Jordan, Capt Thomas	7
Houston, Hugh	61	Jordan, Thomas	75
Houston, William	29	Julian, Charles	87
How, Richard	12	Keays, James	59
Howard, Benjamin	4,5,83	Keeling, Andrew	29
Howard, Dr Ephraim	42,49	Kellor, George	92
Howard, Ephraim	70	Kelly, William	11,70
Howard, Henry	42,49,70	Kemble, Emanuel	47
Howard, John	44	Kempton, Samuel	24,86
Howard, Sarah	48	Kenner, Matthew	59,62
Howlett, John	92	Kennerly, James	61
Hoye, Daniel	78	Kenton, Mark	77
Hughes, Billy	50	Kerr, Edward	86
Hughes, Emory	46	Kilty, John	89
Hughes, William	40	Kinchler, Peter	48
Huison, Capt	25	Kirk, James	43,75
Hunter, James	68	Kirkwood, John	78
Hurley, John	48	Knapp, Frances	11
Hurst, Edward	35	Knowles, John	43
Hutchings, Robert	5,61	Knox, Alexander	37
Hutchings, Capt Thomas	3,22,31,86	Knox, Sarah	41,92
Ingalls, Thomas	25,81	La Girouette	21

Supplementary Runaways Index

Laderdale, James	39	Lyon, Robert	21
Laird, James	18	MacCubbin, Zachariah	74
Lambuth, Samuel	38	Mackay, Patrick	66,87
Lane, Hardage	22,60	Mackey, George	52
Lane, James	32	Mackue, John	55
Lane, John	87	Maginess, James	18
Lane, Capt William	31	Magruder, Nathaniel	68
Lane, William	9,49,	Mallory, Phillip	91
Lane, William Carr	57	Marmaduke, William	74
Langham, James	29	Marr, John	91
Langstone, Matthew	46	Martin, John	14
Langton, Anthony	10	Mascall, Thomas	54
Laverty, James	21	Mason, Lieut	24
Lawson, Thomas	13,33,51,57,70,75	Mason, John	11
Leadbeater, John	51	Massie, Capt Thomas	63
Lee, Philip Ludwell	7	Massie, Thomas	49
Lee, Richard	17,25,67,85	Massy, Edward	83
Lee, Richard Henry	92	Mathews, George	8,32,48,54,82
Leitch, Andrew	27,63,65	Mathews, Sampson	8,32,54,82
Leitch, John	1	Mathews, Sampson	32
Lenox, Walter	54	Mathews, Sampson	54
Lenox, Walter	88	Mathews, Sampson	82
Leslie, George	16	Mathison, David	54
Lester, Thomas	42	Matthews, Archer	72,75
Lewis, Col Fielding	76	Matthews, George	6,9,27,36,47,59,65,66* 69,78*,82*,85
Lewis, John	5,50,58,82		
Lewis, Capt Richard	21,22,35,42,46,76	Matthews, Sampson	6,7,27,47,65,66*,69,78*,85
Lewis, Thomas	65	Mattox, William	55
Libiter, John	50	Maxey, Edward	63
Lightfoot, William	7,90	Maxwell, John	19,89
Lindsay, Capt John	72	May, John	59
Linton, Lieut William	13,23,46,53*	Mayes, Matthew Jr	17
Lipscomb, Capt Reuben	2,42	Mayo, John	26
Lipscomb, Reuben	6*,8,34,64,67,68,88,89	McAboy, Murthy	35
Lipscombe, Daniel	6	McCall & Shedden	28,70
Llewellin, Thomas	1	McCall, Archibald	34
Llewellyn, Thomas	85	McCarty, Capt	48,54
Lloyd, Nicholas	55	McCarty, Charles	16,38,47
Lockhart, Patrick	45,50,82,	McCaul, Archibald	3
Lomberd, Samuel	77	McClure, Andrew	71
Long, Samuel	32	McDaniel, James	56
Lorrain, Barnabas	56	McDonald, Edward	21
Lowes, Capt James	75	McDonald, John	76
Ludlow, Capt	28	McCall & Shedden	70
Lyle, James	35,44	McDowall, James	27*,56,57,80,90
Lyne, John	14,19,24,25,76	McDowell, J	55,57
Lynn, John	9	McDowell, Samuel	44
Lynn, Robert	73	McDowgal, John	21
Lynn, Dr William	35	McGuier, Thomas	35
Lynn, William	13	McIntyre, Capt Alexander	76
Lynton, Anthony	7	McKendrick, Archibald	63
		McKittrick, Robert	82

Supplementary Runaways Index

Name	Pages
McLachlin, John	16
Meade, Capt R.K.	24
Meek, Andrew	56
Mercer, John	13,15,85
Meredith, William	42
Meroney, James	57
Merritt, Matthias	14
Michum, Thomas	73,74
Middleton, Anne	20
Midlimist, Archibald	59
Miller, James	7,80
Miller, Thomas	26,44
Mills, James	79
Minitree, Jacob Andrew	24,37,51
Mitchell, James	11,12,14,30,72,78
Mitchell, Stephen	72
Money, Nicholas	58
Montgomerie, Thomas	2
Moody, Edward	53
Mooney, Nicholas	58
More, Robert	77
Morgan, Daniel	19,92
Morgan, Capt Henry	17
Morgan, Nathaniel	6
Morrison, William	59
Morton, Joseph	82,85
Moseley, Hillary	83
Mountgomery, James	15
Mountjoy, John	90
Muirhead, John	2
Mulligan, Hercules	74
Murphey, Francis	70
Murphree, John	30
Murphy, James	47
Murrill, George	69
Muse, James	54
Muter, Capt George	31,54
Muter, George	42
Nabb, John	17
Neale, Shapleigh	32
Neill, Lewis	45,53
Neilson, Charles	47
Nelson, Capt	21
Netherlan, Wade	42*
Nevett, Thomas	1,4,36,61,75,84
Nevill, John	43,71
Newton, James	25
Newton, Willoughby	5
Nicolson, Robert	4
Nivet, Capt	26
Nixon, Jonathan	77,78
Norris, Benjamin Bradford	74
North & Sands	47
North, Roger	52
Norton, John	87
Norvell, George	56
O'Brian, John	9
Oakes, Charles	35
Ord, Ralph	80
Orm, John	3
Orr, John	29
Orton, Reginald	73
Overton, Lieut Thomas	12,15,46,64,76
Owen, Jeremiah	13
Owl, John	49
Oxen, William	67
Page, Martha	62
Pajer, Capt	13
Pannill, Joseph	3,13,27,29,34,47,55*,62,68,73*
Park, Capt	71
Parker, Isaac	67
Parks, William	88,92
Parrot, Thomas	70
Parsons, James	47
Pascal, Henry	11,51,53,54
Pate, Thomas	2
Paterson, Ann	63
Patteson, James	63
Pattie, James	46
Patton, Capt Thomas	47
Payne, Capt	73
Peachey, Lieut-Col William	81
Peachey, William	36,80
Peak, William	37
Pearce, Mary	40
Pearce, Peter	40
Pearce, William	65
Peirce, Joseph	37
Pelham, Capt	76
Pelham, Peter	16,25,47,52,56,72,80
Perfect, Christopher	62
Perkins, Ensign Harden	31,46
Peyton, Capt Yelverton	76
Peyton, Francis	81
Philips, Mary	21
Phillips, Francis	38,79
Phillips, Richard	42,82
Phillips, Robert	1,44,52,90
Phoset, Thomas	28
Pierce, Capt Joseph	3
Pierce, Joseph	81
Pierce, William	81

Supplementary Runaways Index

Name	Pages	Name	Pages
Pierce, William Jr	41*,89,90	Richardson, John	12
Pleasants, John	45,71*	Riddick, Lemuel	64
Pollard, Thomas	43	Rigden, Thomas	24,71
Pollard, William	18,60	Riggs, Thomas	40
Popjee, William	65	Ritchie, Thomas	24,64
Porter, Benjamin	57	Roane, William	58
Porter, William	26	Rob, James	15
Portlock, Samuel	28,67	Roberts, Charles	59
Powel, Levin	4	Roberts, John	53
Powell, James	21	Roberts, Lemuel	26
Poythress, Joshua	63	Robertson, Moses	5
Poythress, Robert	11	Robins, Thomas	43,92
Presly, Peter	75	Robinson, Capt	12
Pretlow, Samuel	7	Robison, John	71
Pretlow, Thomas	7	Rooke, Bartholomew	36
Price, Thomas	73,74	Rooke, Capt Bartholomew	83
Pride, James	4,35	Rootes, George	60
Pugh, Theophilus	22	Rose, Alexander	56
Purcell, John	22,35	Rose, Rev Robert	35,56
Purdie & Dixon	13	Ross, David	27
Pursell, Anthony	62	Row, William	20
Purvis, John	50	Rowand, Thomas	88
Putterill, Thomas	67	Rowntree, Capt William	16,19,21,26,27,30,32*,3
Quarles, John Jr	2		60,68,72,73,81,87,89*,9
Quinn, Richard	11	Royston, Richard Wiatt	72
Rainbord, Jessath	67	Ruff, William	40
Ralls, John	17	Ruffin, Capt	37
Ramsay, Capt	63	Russel, John	19,41
Ramsay, Alexander	15	Rutherford, Robert	41,55
Ramshire, Mary	67	Sale, Cornelius	6
Rand, William	29	Saunders, John	22
Randall, John	26	Saunders, Thomas	8
Randolph, Peter	43	Saunders, William	2
Randolph, Ry.	38	Schoolar, John	58
Rayson, Capt	67	Scott, Samuel	39
Reaburn, Adam	14	Scruggs, Gross	30,39,63
Read, Coleman	54	Seabrook, Nicholas Brown	82
Reader, Robert	16	Sears, Richard	26
Redman, Francis	68	Sears, William	79
Redmond, Francis	68	Searson, Francis	63
Redurgam, Nathaniel	53	Self, William	74
Reed, John	4,70	Sell, George	59,86
Renick, William	37	Settle, William	9,33
Rennolds, Robert	17	Sharpe, Sgt John	76
Revers, Robert	70	Shedden, William	14
Reynolds, David	54	Sheild, Robert	66
Reynolds, Thomas	69	Shiels, Robert	75
Reynolds, William	82,87	Shipard, John	56,78
Rhoades, Thomas	21	Shippey, John	49,68
Rhodes, Thomas	19,27		
Richards, William	90	**SHIPS**:	
		Alexandria	3

Supplementary Runaways Index

Allerton	2	Norfolk's Revenge	14
American Congress	5,7,58,63,92	Occoquan	56,75
Anne	27,84	Polly	74,78
Baltimore	12	Prince William	12
Becky	10,18,51,78	Queensborough	2
Berry	10,56,79	Rachael	50
Betsy	26,63,69,80.83	Rachel	34
Billy	13	Raleigh	53
Brilliant	20.80	Revenge	13,90
Burwell	25	Sally	84
Carlisle	25	Scorpion	12,22,51,63*,68
Castle	28,52,90	Smith	3
Catherine	47	St Bees	50
Chance	33,48,88	Success's Increase	4,25,27
Delight	36,83	Susanna	31,46
Donald	27*,56.57,80,90	Theodorick	1
Douglas	93	Triton	35,47,68,83,
Duke of Argyl	28	Vernon	10
Duke of Cumberland	3,49,66	Virginian	21,22,35,42,46
Dutchess of Queensbury	47	Vulture	7
Elizabeth	29,63,70,80,81,91	Walpole	92
Encouragement	44,49,58,75	Washington	83
Essex	17	Wilcox	43
Fairfield	58,89	William & Anne	27
Fortune	16,19,21,26,27,0,32*,38,40,	Shipwith, Sir Payton	16
	60,68,72,73,81,87,89*,91	Short, Isaac	18
Fowey	24,55	Shortwell, John	20
Friendship	71	Silbey, John	87
Greenvale	24	Simmons, Isaac	68
Hanbury	62	Simpson, Alexander	75
Hannah	45	Simpson, Joseph	39,66
Hector	76	Simpson, Robert	67
Hero	31,42,54,70,78	Sinclaire, George	64
Hodgson	13	Singleton, Daniel	45,66
Hope	66	Singleton, Menoah	45,66
Hoyne	33,36,44,71	Skinner, Darby	84
Industrious Bee	11,51,53,54	Smeddle, Richard	75
Industry	75	Smith, Capt	50,78,79,84,90
Innermay	45	Smith, Anne	69
Jenny	78	Smith, Capt Archibald	49,84
John & Mary	33	Smith, Augustine	60
King of Prussia	71	Smith, Edward	29
Lark	72	Smith, Edward	80
Liberty	67	Smith, Francis	57,68,88,89
London	5	Smith, Francis Sr	3
Lord Camden	16,19,92	Smith, Francis Jr	71
Lord Stanley	53	Smith, Frederick	46
Manly	2	Smith, Gregory	55
Maryland Merchant	7	Smith, Col John	72
Molly	1,27,30,33	Smith, John Jr	72
Muskito	24,57,86	Smith, Lieut Matthew	76
Nassau	8		

Supplementary Runaways Index

Smith, Philip	52*	Sullivane, Margaret	17
Smith, Capt William	12,26,47	Sumner, Jethro	26
Smith, William	85	Sumner, Luke	11
Smithson, William	1,15	Syme, Col John	28,67
Snowden, Richard	17,34,73	Syme, John	33,43,92
Somerville, Capt	82	Taite, William	22,41,62
Soul, John	77	Taliaferro, Richard	66
Sournas, Mary	31	Taliaferro, William	50
Sournas, Nicholas	31	Tayloe, Col	70
Southall, James*	32	Tayloe, Hon John	13,79
Spain, Isaac	79	Tayloe, John	56,69
Spencer, Capt	49	Taylor, Francis	9
Spencer, Joseph	9,49	Taylor, James	37
Spender, Capt	9	Taylor, Miles	11,28
Spicer, Randolph	40	Taylor, Policarpus	24,55
Spotswood, Col Alexander	10,17,22,23,25,45,51,52,67*, 73,79*,83	Taylor, Ralph	62
		Taylor, Richard	17
Sprigg, Richard	48	Tebbs, Foushee	35
Springate, William	77	Terrell, Capt Harry	54,72
Spruce, Apswell	77	Terrill, Edmund	36
St George, H.U.	75	Terry, Nathaniel	61
Stabler, Edward	64	Tharp, Matthew	61
Stafford, Dr John	36	Thomas, Francis	43,52
Stagg, Mrs	74	Thompson, James	27,84
Stahan, Capt	27	Thompson, William	64
Standford, Joseph	66	Thorn, Widow	34
Stanton, John	91	Thornbery, Samuel	49,68
Stark, W	15	Thornton, Anthony Jr	10
Staunton, John	78	Thorp, Thomas	58
Steel, William	78	Tinsley, William	55
Steuart, George	6	Tippett, John	85
Steuart, John	33	Todd, William	39
Stevens, Samuel	48	Tomkies, Capt Charles	6*,8,23,34,64,67,68,8
Stevenson, Edward	7,59,61,65,73,86,89,92	Tomkies, Francis	51
Stevenson, John	60	Tool, Darby	20
Stevenson, Robert	46	Toone, James	7
Steward, William	53	Topin, John	83
Stewart, David	12	Towell, John	81
Stewart, Dr George	76	Towers, John	25
Stewart, Elizabeth	86	Travis, Edward	30,91
Stewart, Walter	30	Trebell, William	40
Stobo, Robert	20,28,40	Trebell, William	63
Storrs, Joshua	16	Trimble, John	26
Street, Capt Joseph	57	Triplett, Francis	59
Stretch, John	6	Triplet, William	25
Stringer, John	79	Tuberville, George	19,44,54,62
Strother, Mr	39	Tuberville, John	3,13,16,17,19,86
Strother, Anthony	28	Turner, Thomas	35,65
Strother, John	1	Tutt, James	60
Strother, Joseph	3	Valentine, Jacob	24,57,86
Struther, John	54	Vaulx, Robert	3,41,91
Stuart, John	56		

Supplementary Runaways Index

Name	Pages	Name	Pages
Wade, Elizabeth	7	Willits, Samuel	26
Wadling, James	85	Willman, Matthew	9
Waggoner, Capt Thomas	9,32,75	Willmore, Sarah	91
Wales, Andrew	83	Wills, Micajah	33
Walke, Anthony	42	Wilson, Capt	18
Walker, Alice	26	Wilson, John	31,62,78,79
Walker, Robert	62	Wilson, John William	91
Walker, William	26,48	Wilson, Sarah	48
Wallace, James	2,85	Wilson, Thomas	40
Wallace, Robert	11,35,51	Wise, Peter	39
Walton, George	1,15,18,58,71,82,91	Withers, William	10,26,60
Walton, Robert	1,15,18,58,71,82,91	Wood, James	71
Ward, Lieut Robert	12,23*,34,78,91	Wood, Samuel	57*
Warricker, William	86	Woods, Richard	16,18
Warton, Thomas	88	Woodside, John	65
Washington, General	62	Woodward, Henry	9,32,76
Washington, Augustine	48,54	Woolsey, George	72,81
Washington, George	77,87	Worley, Caleb	19,34,45
Washington, John Augustine	3,13,16,17,19	Wormeley, John	81
Washington, Lawrence Sr	16	Wortham, James	76
Washington, Samuel	90	Wright, Joseph	53
Waters, James	84	Wright, Westcott	51
Watkins, Henry	66	Wyatt, William	20,52,62,82
Watkins, Joseph	6	Wylie, Hugh	1
Watkins, Thomas	36	Yates, Robert	28,42
Watson, William	8	Younghusband, Capt Isaac	24
Wayman, John	87	Zane, Isaac	50,58,88
Webb, William	8		
Wellman, Matthew	46		
Welsh, Benjamin	40		
West, John	68		
Westcott, Wright	12,22,63*,68		
Wheatley, Anne	89		
White, Bennett	20,31		
White, David	89		
White, Lieut Tarpley	2,22,23,42,52		
Whitehead, William	83		
Whiting, Thomas	41		
Whitley, Robert	19,89		
Whitwell, Matthew	35,68,83		
Whitworth, Sir Charles	60		
Wignall, Capt	8		
Willcock, William	51		
Williams, Henry	90		
Williams, Mary	42		
Williams, Thomas	34		
Williams, William	28,82		
Williamson, Thomas	62		
Willis, Francis	16		
Willis, Col Henry	48		
Willis, Thomas	48		

CPSIA information can be obtained at www.ICGtesting.com
Printed in the USA
BVOW05s1511121115
426784BV00009B/136/P